CULTURE SHOCK
and
TIGER BOMBS
*tales of living in Sri Lanka
(and other countries too)*

Harry Marcus

PublishAmerica
Baltimore

© 2011 by Harry Marcus.
All rights reserved. No part of this book may be reproduced, stored in a retrieval system or transmitted in any form or by any means without the prior written permission of the publishers, except by a reviewer who may quote brief passages in a review to be printed in a newspaper, magazine or journal.

First printing

PublishAmerica has allowed this work to remain exactly as the author intended, verbatim, without editorial input.

Hardcover 978-1-4560-6070-1
Softcover 978-1-4560-6071-8
PUBLISHED BY PUBLISHAMERICA, LLLP
www.publishamerica.com
Baltimore

Printed in the United States of America

To Uncle Steve
and
Aunty Sue,

I hope you enjoy the book. I'm expecting to be invited onto the Oprah Book-club any day now.

Merry Xmas!

'Harry Marcus'

1
Colombo, Sri Lanka, February 2010

    A commotion outside drew me to the window this morning and I watched impassively as a young boy struggled to shove a fully grown goat into a brown hessian sack in the street below me. The usual neighbourhood characters had stopped what they were doing and gathered round to watch, laugh and shout advice. The young boy shouted something in Sinhalese as the goat resisted and jumped around in circles on the end of a piece of rope. Amid much tangling the boy finally wrestled the goat to the ground, pinned it down with his knee and punched it in the belly to a chorus of laughs and cheers from the adults watching in the street. He shoved the goat backwards into his sack before he hoisted it over his shoulder and stomped off up the street in a bad mood.

    Three years ago I would have been enthralled by this little scene, but I have grown so used to the unexpected and bizarre dramas of life in Sri Lanka that a boy shoving a goat into a sack no longer surprises me. I have lived in Colombo for three years now and scenes like this no longer make me smile. Sri Lanka is a crazy place and it has finally worn me down.

    This is a familiar feeling. The same thing has happened in all the countries we have lived in. My wife, Mary, and I have lived overseas for the last twenty years, in six different countries, and on each occasion I started off loving the country and ended up hating it. I used to think that I was on some sort of regular, repeating cycle of joy, anger then depression, but I recently found an article that put forward a more comforting explanation.

The article explained that there are four distinct phases of culture shock that anyone who moves to a new country goes through. The first phase is fascination: an initial period when everything is new and exciting and there are seemingly few problems because the predominant feeling is one of exhilaration. It is like being on an extended vacation. The second phase is friendship, where new social bonds are formed to replace the ones left behind. Your new friends, whether fellow expatriates or natives of the country, become invaluable gurus who advise you on everything: schools, where to shop, what to buy, where to live and so on. The third phase is frustration. This phase usually only affects long term expats that have been in the country long enough to get over the excitement of everything being new. Anger and irritation take over as the reality of life in a strange place begins to kick in. Hostility to the local people, and particularly those who are in authority, becomes the predominant emotion. Finally, there is the fourth stage, fulfilment. You accept your new environment for what it is, you compromise and adapt to local culture. You are at peace in your adopted home.

I like this theory because it fits with what has happened to me. I was not crazy, I was going through phases of culture shock. According to the article, everyone who moves to a new country goes through it. Granted, I did not follow the process exactly, because it seems clear to me that I always got stuck in phase three, annoyed and irritated by things that went wrong in the country. But I think I know why that is. I never reached the contented, fulfilled stage because we lived in such bizarre places where things always went wrong. If we had moved to more developed, western style cities, say, San Francisco,

Vienna, Sydney, or even Hong Kong or Singapore, then I am sure I would have had a very short period of phase three followed by a long and contented period of phase four. But we only visited nice, modern cities on holiday, as a respite from the day-to-day turmoil of living in Montevideo, Jeddah, Nairobi, Abidjan, Bridgetown and now Colombo.

In a recent Mercer study that ranked the biggest 202 cities in the world by their quality of life, Abidjan came in 195, just a few places above Baghdad. Jeddah was ranked 162, Nairobi at 156, and Colombo at 136. Montevideo came in at a relatively lofty 76, while Bridgetown was presumably considered too small and insignificant to rate. Bridgetown apart, it is probably fair to say that where we have lived would not be on most people's list of a place to spend extended period of time. And believe me, the reality of life in Bridgetown is nothing like a sun and sand beach holiday.

The website Expat Exchange is a good site, designed to help people when they first move overseas, giving useful tips and advice of how to cope when you move to a new country. The website carries the following quote:

'Carpe Diem; live life to the full and enjoy all the fantastic opportunities of living in another city and culture. Keep things in perspective and try not to let your pleasure be affected by the inevitable irritations of living in an unfamiliar world and the bureaucracy of another country. Of course they do things differently'.

It struck me that 'inevitable irritations' is rather a broad category. For example, some people may consider a different language or having to eat unfamiliar food an irritation. Perhaps having to deal with unnecessary bureaucracy is an 'inevitable irritation'. But this is completely subjective. What would Expat Exchange make of some of things that have irritated me over the years? Things such as: long power cuts, water shortages, suicide bombers, public disorder and civil war, terrorist attacks, dangerous driving, totalitarian governments and dictators, zero customer service, health problems, hot and oppressive weather and a complete lack of familiar goods, amenities, food and facilities. Would Expat Exchange still refer to these things as mere 'irritations'? I accept that some people may cope with these things better than I do, but I think you have to accept that there is a world of difference between being irritated by a new country's strange food and by, say, three weeks without any water coming out of the tap. After a couple of years of that sort of thing, it does become very hard to shrug your shoulders, ignore them and get on with your life unaffected. So, easier said than done, Expat Exchange.

I realise it is all a balancing act. If you can let the irritations go then there is more room to enjoy the unpredictable events that life in a different country can bring. During a short ten minute gaze out of the window this morning I saw not only the boy shove a goat in a sack, I also watched a succession of red tuc-tucs trundle past on the dusty road with their small, distinctive noisy engines, with the drivers leaning out and whistling and trying to entice passengers. I heard the single strike of the bell at the Buddhist temple at the end of our street and I heard the local fish seller shout 'malu' (Singhalese for 'fish') before he freewheeled at speed on his bicycle into our street, grinning, barefoot and bare chested, followed by a dozen street cats sprinting desperately to catch up for some scraps from the ice box of tuna and swordfish wired to the back of his bicycle.

I forget sometimes that these sights and sounds are quite unusual if you do not happen to live in a small side street in Borella, a suburb of Colombo, in Sri Lanka, in the South Asian tropics.

2

Colombo, as all the guidebooks will tell you, is a bit on the ugly side. Of course the militarisation of the city does not help its aesthetic appeal, but even if you allow for that, the city has few redeeming landmarks. Probably the most important aspect of the city is its huge natural harbour. Colombo has an important strategic position in the East-West sea trade routes and if you wander down to the sea front anywhere along the west coast you can see a long line of container ships heading from the East, from Hong Kong and Singapore, to call in on Colombo before continuing around the Arabian peninsular through the Suez canal and on to Europe. It says a lot about Colombo I think when the view of a long, singular line of container ships is one of the more interesting features of the city. More generally, Colombo is all pollution, exhaust fumes, ugly concrete architecture stained black from the rains, beggars on street corners, potholes, broken pavements and huge and tasteless advertising boards for mobile phones and a sugary drink called 'Smak'. There is no point in trying to dress it up, Colombo is ugly.

From my Western perspective, the familiar lives alongside the alien. The colonial past is evident in the street names: Flower

Road, Prince of Wales Avenue and Union Place; and they form prominent arteries through the city alongside more daunting pronunciations of street names like Sri Jayawardenepura Mawatha, Dudley Senanayake Mawatha and Thimbirigaysaya Road. There are elite local private schools with expansive cricket grounds, called Royal College, St Thomas' or St Joseph's, but they are uniquely Sri Lankan, they have no pretensions to be British and follow their own curriculums. And if you find the local dishes too hot and spicy there are branches of McDonalds; but alongside Big Macs and fries you can order a McCurry and McRice.

Outside the capital city, Sri Lanka is quite different: more scenic, full of natural, underdeveloped jungle lowlands and picturesque tea plantations in the hills. The beaches of the south coast near Galle and the hill country around Kandy are particularly beautiful areas that could, with the right development, generate a lucrative tourism industry. As it stands, however, tourism is in formative development at best, and that is because most people do not associate Sri Lanka with holidays and natural beauty. Sri Lanka is better known as a country at war with itself. For three decades, war and terrorism has wrecked any prospect of economic progress on the island as the two main groups of people in Sri Lanka, the Singhalese and the Tamils, have fought a prolonged war against each other.

The reasons behind the war are not particularly complex. When Sri Lanka became independent in 1948 the main protagonists behind the freedom movement were Singhalese and they aimed to make Sri Lanka a Singhalese nation-state. They enacted a new 'Sinhala Only Act' that mandated that the language of the Singhalese was to become the new sole official language of the new country, replacing English, which had previously provided a common language for the Singhalese and Tamils to communicate in. The Singhalese saw the measure as a way of distancing themselves from their colonial past, but they were equally aware that the Act would mean that large numbers of Tamils who worked in the civil service would not meet the new language requirement and would be forced to resign. As an additional measure, the Singhalese introduced affirmative action so that Singhalese workers were hired at the expense of Tamils, to reverse what they saw as colonial favouritism in employing Tamils. Further legislation cut Tamil places at universities and declared that Buddhism had 'foremost place' in Sri Lanka at the expense of the Tamil religion of Hinduism.

The driving force behind this was the Singhalese claim that Sri Lanka had been a Buddhist nation from historical times, a sort of Buddhist Promised Land, where the Sinhalese should rule and Buddhism should be unchallenged. This philosophy came from a third century book of scripture called the Mahavamsa, written by Buddhist monks in Sri Lanka at the time when Buddhism was being replaced by Hinduism throughout India. The monks established links between the Buddha and Sri Lanka, claiming that Buddha had visited the island three times, and this divine link helped to maintain Sri Lanka as Buddhism's last remaining outpost in the subcontinent. In addition, many Singhalese believed the legend of the tooth relic: that the right to rule the land was directly linked to the custodianship of a tooth, believed to have been taken from the funeral pyre of the Buddha. Although, during their colonial period in the sixteenth century, the Portuguese unsportingly seized what they thought was the relic and burnt it with Catholic fervour, the Singhalese later claimed that they had in fact stolen a replica. The real tooth, according to believers, had been guarded since the seventeenth century at the Temple of the Sacred Tooth in Kandy, and had even been hidden away safely by a senior monk during the British occupation of the island during the nineteenth and twentieth centuries. These beliefs fostered a kind of intolerant chauvinism amongst the Singhalese and a real sense of entitlement, that they were the only true guardians of their island.

In response to this deliberate marginalisation, many Tamils began to think that they deserved a separate nation-state for themselves and the geographical concentration of the two groups helped to push this idea forward. Singhalese people make up around 75 per cent of the Sri Lankan population and they are mainly situated in the south and centre of the island. The Tamils make up around 12 per cent of the nation's population and they are mainly in the north and the east. In some places Tamils are in the clear majority: for example, the city of Jaffna on the north coast is 95 per cent Tamil. The LTTE (Liberation Tigers of Tamil Eelam) or as they are more commonly known in the West, the Tamil Tigers, began to fight for what they believed was the only way to guarantee themselves a life without discrimination, the creation of an independent state called Eelam in the north and east of the island. This was opposed by the Singhalese spiritually because of their belief that Sri Lanka was divinely theirs by right, and practically, because they believed that the island was too small to be carved up into two and that the Tamils were claiming too much land as their own.

The tension between the two groups led to increased violence and sporadic attacks, until, the watershed moment in 1983 that is often credited as being the start of the civil war. The LTTE attacked and killed a convoy of 15 government soldiers near Jaffna and when the news reached Colombo there was a dramatic anti-Tamil backlash. Mobs equipped with voter registration lists burned down Tamil homes and businesses in Colombo and violently attacked Tamils in the streets with bars and bats, dragging people from cars and buses. There were accusations that the government were actively engaged in organising the attacks and that the police stood by and did little to intervene. In the Colombo prison, over fifty Tamils were killed by Singhalese inmates when the guards claimed that cell keys had been stolen from them, not once, but twice in two separate attacks. The government said that in total 250 Tamils had been killed, but estimates from international agencies put the number at closer to 4,000. In addition, because their homes had been torched, there were close to 50,000 homeless Tamil refugees in Colombo. They were housed in temporary shelters for months until eventually they were shipped north by the government, with help from the Indian government. To this day no compensation has been paid and no criminal charges have been brought against anyone involved in the massacres. To the Tamils the event is known as 'Black July': thousands of them were forced to either flee the country or move to a new home in the north, increasing further the concentration of Tamils in that part of Sri Lanka. The LTTE recruited many disillusioned and angry young recruits and the armed struggle began in earnest. The result was almost thirty years of atrocities on both sides in which most estimates put the death toll at close to 100,000 people.

    Last year, in a gruesome final push for victory, the Singhalese Government forces finally defeated the Tamil Tigers. The consequences of the victory are unknown at the moment, but if there is a genuine desire for national reconciliation then Sri Lanka should surely see development like its neighbours in India, Malaysia and Thailand. As things stand, the country is decades behind. Even for someone middle aged like me, Colombo feels sleepy and tired. Travel from here to somewhere else in the region, be it Bangkok, Delhi or Singapore, and you are confronted with enterprise and energy. In Colombo, the streets are virtually empty at 9pm. There is no music, no lights and no excitement. It is no surprise that the tourists that visit Sri Lanka tend to miss out the capital completely and head straight to the beaches of the south coast. I recently saw a book called '1,000 places to see before you die' and I was tempted to buy it because I noticed it had a section on Colombo. However, the Colombo section consisted of just one entry: the Galle Face Hotel. The Galle Face is a mildly interesting, run-down, colonial-era building by the sea front. We go there occasionally because you can sit on their terrace and have a drink overlooking the

Indian Ocean while being served by men sporting big, waxed moustaches in white shorts, long socks and funny hats. However, the Galle Face hotel is also right next to the Sri Lankan Army headquarters, and it is therefore the most heavily guarded and militarised zone in the city. The street outside is full of armoured tanks and military checkpoints. Soldiers speed by in jeeps and point their guns at the passersby. Others watch from their watchtowers surrounded by razor wire, keeping an eye on the people below. Soldiers stand around on the streets pointing guns and demanding to see ID papers. If you wander outside the confines of the hotel you are immediately surrounded by military hardware. Given the number of rifles that swivel and point at you in that part of town, the Galle Face Hotel would be better included in a book entitled '1,000 places to see just moments before you die'.

3

I have no job here, unless you count being a househusband a job, which I have noticed, most people do not. We came to Sri Lanka when Mary signed a contract to work as an English teacher. I had recently quit my job working for the British Foreign Office, the equivalent of the US State Department, and I knew that I would be without work in Sri Lanka, but Mary and I are as bad as each other when the chance to live in a new country presents itself. We cannot resist the adventure. We moved out here with our young son Sam, who was six when we arrived and who is now nearly nine, and we began our new life in the tropics. Mary's contract is up in less than six months and we have no idea where we will move to next.

This is the first time that Mary has been the earner and I have accompanied her overseas. My wife's employer refers to me as a 'trailing spouse', which I find mildly offensive, although I admit it is fairly accurate. At least when I worked for the Foreign Office, they had the good grace to refer to Mary as an 'accompanying spouse'.

My life involves shopping cooking and looking after Sam so I am living the life of the stereotypical expat wife, except without the house staff. In contrast to most of the other expats we know (including us, when I was abroad in the diplomatic service), we do not employ a maid, a cook, a nanny, a driver and a gardener. For one thing, our house is too small, but even if we lived in a mansion I would not fancy the idea of playing the master to a collection of house staff. Unfortunately, I am not the perfectionist that Mary is when it comes to tidiness, and accumulated house mess meant that she soon insisted that we hired someone to clean up once a week. So, we employed a housemaid called Sukunthala, or Kunty for short. I really do not care if she can clean or not, anyone called Kunty needs a break in life.

With the contract due to end we really need to decide what to do next. Mary could apply for new jobs teaching English, even stay with her existing employer, but we would need to be transferred to a different country. This would be a continuation of what we have always known: three years here, three years there. However, the employer will not pay school fees, (which discriminates against those with school age kids, does it not?) and that means that many cities, and by that I mean the nice, modern cities in the world, are too expensive for us. We would need to limit our selection to cities in South Asia, Africa or the Arabian peninsula, and a quick perusal of the upcoming jobs vacancy list shows that jobs in Bangladesh, Sudan and Iraq are on the horizon. I am not thrilled with that lineup. I know that I will reach phase three of 'culture shock' pretty quickly in those places. In fact, I am starting to have doubts about all this moving around more generally. It has increasingly crossed my mind that perhaps it is time to settle down somewhere. I think our son Sam would probably prefer some stability in a modern country. I am in my mid-forties and I am beginning to think that maybe a life in the first world, where things work, would be an agreeable life change. Twenty years ago I would have jumped at the chance of a tour of duty in the Sudan, but now, despite Mary's enthusiasm, it does not appeal at all.

CULTURE SHOCK AND TIGER BOMBS

Yet even if we decide to swap our nomadic life for a more permanent home, we still need to decide where that may be. After living overseas for twenty years, 'home' becomes a vague concept. Mary's mantra for many years has been 'home is where your stuff is'. In any case, my notional home is in northern England and Mary's is in Wisconsin in America. Sam was born in Ireland. Where do we retreat to if we give up our life of hopping from country to country?

Our house in Colombo is pretty unusual by western standards, but quite common in Sri Lanka. We live on a small side street in Borella, or Colombo 8, as all the locals snappily call it, in the top half of a large old house while our Sri Lankan landlords, Aravinda and Amali, live underneath. Lots of houses are built like this so that extended families can live together but still preserve a degree of privacy. There are three houses in our little street and they are all set up in this way, with parents underneath and their kids and grandkids on the top floor. Aravinda and Amali's kids are both studying in Melbourne, so we get to rent their place until they decide to return - if they ever do. Their eldest kid, Sampath has really been spreading out his studies. I think he has been there for nearly seven years now. I think his plan is to stay there long enough to qualify for an Australian passport.

I was very suspicious of signing up for a home when the landlord lives underneath, but Aravinda and Amali have both been very accommodating and friendly. They fix things very promptly when they break, mainly because Aravinda is the manager of a tea factory and he simply hauls people off the production line to come to our place and, for example, fix the washing machine. They are also very sociable and they invite us downstairs to drink arrack, (a coconut based alcohol that tastes a bit like rum) and eat Sri Lankan food with our fingers. Unlike us, they have an army of deferential house staff to serve drinks, cook food and clean up afterwards.

Our flat, or top half of a house, I am not sure which is the more appropriate term, is a bit run down, with tatty furnishings, kitchen cupboard doors that keep falling off, and an electrical supply that blows light bulbs at a rate of three a week, but we like it. The home is so old and temperamental that we have simply adjusted to a completely new way of living. For example, our cooker does not warm up properly and produces an incredibly foul odour whenever it is switched on, so we have stopped using it and cook all our food on a single gas hob camping stove instead. (It takes impressive coordination to cook a meal that needs more than one thing heated up).

Our pop culture references are all different here: our TV comes direct from India and we now watch all forms of cricket as well as shows like the Little Lord Krishna and India's Got Talent Khoj. Our telephone system is all gnarled wires and loose connections so that every time the phone rings we expect it to be the wrong caller. We get at least four or five wrong calls a day and they always follow the same pattern:

Caller: Hello, (louder) HELLO, (still louder) HELLO?
Me: Can I help you?
Caller: HELLO? HELLO? HELLO?
Me: I think you may have the wrong number.
Caller: Mr. Lamabadusooiya? (or Mr. Wadugadapitiya? or Mr. Gunawardena? etc)
Me: No, I am sure you have the wrong number.
Caller: Click.

Never a 'sorry to bother you', never a 'goodbye', just hang up without a word. Cultural difference, I know, but I find it incredibly rude nonetheless.

Although we live near the centre of town and it is a built up area, the local wildlife seem keen to share our home with us. We wage a constant war against the mosquitoes. We have to close all our windows at 5pm every night, because at dusk the mosquitoes that cause dengue fever and another disease called chikungunya (which I had never even heard of before we came here) come out to bite. Both diseases cause bones and muscles to ache and come with searing fevers. Most people are, needless to say, anxious to avoid dengue and chikungunya and a whole freelance industry has sprung up in Colombo to try and keep the mosquitoes at bay. Men carrying indeterminable chemicals in old, used plastic litre bottles of coca cola with connecting spray guns knock on house doors eager to spray your house in the war on mosquitoes. Such is my paranoia about dengue and chikungunya that I am willing to shell out cash for a stranger to liberally spray my entire house with strange ammonia smelling liquid. He may have siphoned the liquid off from some cesspit for all I know. Others entrepreneurs entice you with big smoke canisters that explode thick white smog fumes that takes hours to clear and kills anything that flies into its path. Yet neither seems to work properly. Chikungunya and dengue are rife in Sri Lanka. Mary is forever teaching extra classes at work to cover for colleagues who are stuck down and often hospitalised by one of the two diseases.

The situation is taken very seriously in Colombo, so much so that a Government minister, Mervyn Silva, recently tied an official to a tree in Colombo because he had not been attending meetings to discuss a dengue fever outbreak. It was all the talk in our street because it happened quite nearby. Apparently, tying people to trees is a traditional punishment in Sri Lanka used to humiliate people. Incidentally, this Minister, Mr Silva is clearly a bit of a hot head with a reputation for causing trouble. He has been accused by civil rights groups of constantly threatening the media. The French organisation 'Reporters Without Borders' described his ministerial appointment as akin to employing 'an arsonist to put out fires'.

Dengue carrying mosquitoes are not even our most dangerous adversary. Just a week or so after moving in, I opened the door to see a fat, five-foot long black snake whip across the doormat at a strikingly impressive pace. Who knew that snakes could move so fast? They seem even more menacing when the realisation dawns that they can probably slither faster than I can run. Since that first snake by the front door we have seen dozens more around the house and around Colombo, and it never gets any less alarming. Just last week, I was sitting on our little roof terrace when a large bright yellow serpent made its way from our roof to a nearby tree branch just a few feet above my head. I have no idea what kind of snake it was, but from my description, most of our friends seem to think it was a rat snake. My mate Rob was once lying under a shady tree on lounger by a hotel swimming pool when he heard a snap above and a bright yellow snake dropped down and landed in his lap. The pool attendants scared the snake away and told Rob that it was a rat snake. Rat snakes, named for the prey they favour, will bite you if provoked but will probably not kill you, which is encouraging, but not completely reassuring.

My big worry is that a snake will get in the house and I would then have to 'deal with it'. Apparently this is not uncommon. The following is full of unintentional innuendo, but a colleague of Mary's once discovered a huge snake in her bedroom when she was undressing for bed, and fearing a bite on her foot or ankle, she tackled the serpent wearing nothing but a pair of knee high leather boots. She eventually killed the snake by hitting it repeatedly over the head with a seven iron.

So far we have been lucky and there have been no snakes inside our house, but we have seen many of them out and about in the city. I once saw one causing havoc on the Galle Road, the main road in Colombo. It was a huge monster, stripy and dangerous looking, making motorcycles swerve and pedestrians scatter and run away screaming. Luckily a bus driver came to the rescue and ran it over, although, I am pretty certain he squashed it under his wheels because he did not see it, rather than out of any sense of civic duty. In fairness, it is sometimes hard to spot snakes until you are right on top of them. I know this because I once ran over the tail of a Russell's viper on my motorbike when I was in the Colombo suburbs. I only found out it was a Russell's viper because I stopped to see what had caused the bump under my wheels and found a snake in an uncontrollable rage on the road. People had gathered round quickly, keeping a respectable distance, and someone told me to be very careful as 'That one is a Russell's, very big danger, sir'. As the snake lunged, people scattered and threw stones until it eventually got off the road and escaped into long grass on the verge. I googled it when I got home and found out that a Russell's viper is a highly irritable snake that can produce enough venom to inflict excruciating pain and death in an adult in just a few hours. If they are highly irritable to begin with, you can imagine what the snake was like after being run over and then having rocks thrown at by a gang of jeering passersby. I pity the next person to encounter that particular snake. In any case, driving on the roads of Colombo is dangerous enough without pissed off Russell's vipers ready pounce on you from the curb.

We live close to the Royal Colombo Golf Course, and when Sam and I walk to school in the morning we pass alongside the sixth hole on a path under the shade of some trees. Halfway along the hole there is a small water hazard where we see the same old man squatting under a tree each day. We always greet each other and he has told me his name, but in fine Sri Lankan tradition it contains at least six syllables so Sam and I call him 'I'll get it' because whenever a ball lands in the water he jumps up and shouts, 'I'll get it!' and the golfers give him a few rupees for returning their ball. One morning he jumped up when he saw us approach and said, 'Mr. Harry, is it that you want to see a cobra?' (For some reason, in Sri Lanka, many expats end up being addressed like this, with a title and first name. My name is Harry Marcus, but I am called 'Mr. Harry' by most Sri Lankans I know. Even my bill from Ceylon Telecom arrives in the post addressed to 'Mr. Harry').

'I'll get it' explained how a big cobra had taken up residence nearby and came out every evening to hunt. During the day it slept in a cavity in the wall that separated the golf course from the cemetery. 'He's in the wall. Just there. Right behind you' he said, as Sam and I instinctively jumped forward. 'I'll get it' ventured forward, wearing nothing but a pair of shorts and carrying a stick, and we all peered into the cobra hole and saw its thick brown and yellow striped body.

'This one is a big cobra' said 'I'll get it'. 'He is at least ten feet long'

Sam and I exchanged nervous glances, and I was busy imagining what a three metre cobra was capable of killing when all of sudden 'I'll get it' began prodding the snake with his stick, telling me that he would 'get the fellow out of his hole' so we could have a better look. I explained fairly hastily, whilst backing Sam and I away even quicker, that we did not want it out of its hole, that maybe we should leave it sleeping and would it not be annoyed at being poked like that? However, 'I'll get it' kept prodding away, smiling and nodding at us, and making the cobra shift around in his den. The snake was undoubtedly annoyed, but thankfully did not stick his poisonous head out and start hissing and spitting at us.

Thereafter for day upon day, on our journey to school, 'I'll get it' made the same grinning comical show of getting his stick and going to the cobra hole as if to prod him out again, and I made the same theatrical 'no please don't' hand movements. Then, just as it was becoming a bit of a tedious morning game, I noticed that oil had been smeared around the hole and the snake was gone. 'I'll get it' told us that one of the golfers had seen the cobra on the sixth tee early one morning and had made a complaint at the clubhouse. The golf course manager had decided that a deadly snake on the course was potentially not good for business, so they had shooed it away by putting oil around its den in the wall.

'It is a splendid good idea because cobras, they do not like the oil and will go someplace else to cause their palavers' said 'I'll get it'.

I agreed with him that it was a good idea to scare away the cobra, but where was it now? Maybe it had just moved onto the next hole? It could be just a few yards further down the course. But 'I'll get it' waved his hands dismissively.

'It is next door now' he said pointing his stick over the wall. 'It is the problem of the cemetery people now. Nothing to do with the golf course'.

I looked at the overgrown grass amongst all the gravestones in the huge cemetery that backed onto the golf course and thought how difficult it would be to track down a cobra in there. Some poor soul is going to get a nasty shock one day when they kneel down to put some flowers next to grandma's grave.

4

I must admit it is an interesting time to be in Sri Lanka. The country has been going through some quite historic changes. Above all, of course, the long civil war has come to an end. However, it is now one year since the end of the hostilities and the country still operates as if it is on red alert. Emergency regulations that have been in force since 1983 are still being enforced and they give the Government the power to detain suspects indefinitely without charge and to curb public meetings and to halt the distribution of certain literature. There seems to be no movement from the government to restore any civil rights. In fact, if any thing, the contrary seems to be true. The army continues to patrol the streets, setting up roadblocks and randomly checking IDs and harassing people; military helicopters fly past regularly, and journalists disappear if they criticise the government in newspapers.

An expat friend of ours who lives near the Parliament in Colombo was temporarily evicted from his home for a week by the Army because they wanted to use it as a base. They marched into his home one night and gave him 24 hours to find somewhere else to live. They offered neither compensation nor an apology and set up a mounted machine gun on his balcony.

We too have been subjected to a pre-dawn raid by the army: they banged on our door at 4am and came straight into our house, rifles at the ready, to check the rooms for terrorists and bomb making equipment. It was not a very thorough check. We could have been housing a squadron of Tamil Tigers and they would not have noticed. However, this happened after the government had already declared victory in their war against the Tamils. I can understand that perhaps I need to compromise my individual freedom in the interests of security while the country is at war, but if the government is ready to declare the war over, then why should the army poke around my house for no good reason? It was not just our house either; they marched through all the houses in our street. No doubt paying particular attention to the homes of anyone not Singhalese. There is no concept of civil liberty here. There is no protection in the form of a warrant if the authorities want to barge inside your house. If the army bang on your door at dawn and want to come in they are going to do it and you cannot stop them.

To add to this mob-handed army behaviour, the Government has turned more ruthless in its handling of dissent or opposition and the President has become increasingly powerful. Mahinda Rajapaksa is not only the President of Sri Lanka; he is the Minister of Defence, Minister of Finance and Minister of Information, and for good measure, his government includes three of his brothers and one of his sons. I read recently that the BBC reckon that the Rajapaksas are responsible for spending more than two-thirds of Sri Lanka's budget. They are a huge political family dynasty.

Mahinda Rajapaksa is a face you recognise quickly in Colombo because his image is on posters everywhere praising his achievements: the construction of a new bridge is thanks to his magnificence the President, or the repaving of the street is thanks to the generosity of his excellence. There is rarely any mention that all of the money to pay for these works is actually coming from a dubious relationship with China. Rajapaksa is usually depicted dressed all in white like some modern day prophet, or he is holding one arm out into the distance like the communist images of Lenin favoured across the old Eastern bloc. He even went to the trouble of having new 1000 Rupee notes issued with a messiah like image of him on the face. As further evidence of his megalomaniac tendencies, he had his followers erect a 40-foot high statue of him by a major roundabout in Colombo just before the elections. Presumably this was just in case the electorate had forgotten who they were going to vote for.

Physically, he looks like a curious mix of Saddam Hussein and the 1970's American golfer Lee Trevino, with a thick black moustache and a Cheshire cat grin. Unfortunately, he acts more like Saddam than Trevino. Scores of journalists have disappeared into the back of white vans, never to be seen again, after writing critical pieces about the President. For example, the journalist Prageeth Eknaligoda wrote an unfavourable piece about the government and two days before the Presidential election, he went missing. In January 2009, the newspaper editor Lasantha Wickrematunge was murdered and he even wrote an editorial, published posthumously, revealing that if something should happen to him, readers should know that it was the Government that was responsible for his death. Media Rights Groups say that Sri Lanka is now one of the most dangerous places for journalists to work. Rajapaksa even had his personal astrologer arrested for making a prediction that he did not care for.

The President can often be seen speeding around Colombo in his armoured Mercedes with blacked out windows. His entourage always includes masses of bodyguards on bikes and jeeps, blasting horns, flashing lights and pointing rifles. It is quite a spectacle, and no one can miss him, because the police always set up temporary roadblocks and make people wait in the sun for up to 30 or 40 minutes at a time so the President can have the road to himself. It always occurred to me that this behaviour would be intolerable in the west and it set such a poor example, but Sri Lankans seemed to accept the inconvenience willingly. In fact, Rajapaksa retains huge support. He is popular with many rural Sri Lankans who identify with his strong man image, and if some people question the manner of his authoritarian government, he has at least brought the awful conflict with the Tamil Tigers to an end.

When the Sri Lankan army defeated the Tamil Tigers in May 2009, Rajapaksa made sure he got the credit, which caused a serious rift with the General who led the army to victory, General Sarath Fonseca. Ironically, to many outside of Sri Lanka there was not much honour in the killing of around 10,000 innocent people in the final push to get the Tiger leadership, (later estimates have put the casualties as high as 30,000 people, but the Sri Lankan government unsurprisingly disputes this). There were many reports of war crimes, of surrendering rebels being shot and Tamil hospitals being targeted by army shells, and the Government actually banned news agencies and aid workers from the area so that there could be no independent reporting.

At the time it seemed to me that there was very little concern from the Singhalese (although there was plenty from Europe and the USA) that so many Tamils had died, and that those who had survived were displaced, malnourished and locked up in concentration camps. It appeared that most Singhalese thought that all the Tamils in the north were terrorists and were therefore legitimate targets. To me, the people in the north were also Sri Lankan. If the Singhalese saw themselves as so different from the Tamils then they were merely acknowledging what the Tamils themselves wanted: a separate identity. To me, it seemed extremely insensitive when the Singhalese basked in their moment of victory with public holidays, victory parades and flags adorning homes, cars, buses and public buildings. As jubilant patriotism took over the south, the people in the north who had not been killed in the fighting were locked up in awful conditions and foreign aid was inexplicably turned away. The President and a number of other politicians starting referring to Sri Lanka as 'The Motherland' which only served to add to the mood of nationalistic fervour.

The feud between Rajapaksa and General Fonseca over who should be the Singhalese hero for defeating the Tamils became worse in the months after the war. Big billboards of a smiling Rajapaksa were erected in Colombo with messages written in quirky English, like the one near the town hall which read: 'Glory to the President who defeated the Tamil Terrorists and astounded the entire Universe!' Fonseca felt like he was not given enough credit for the war effort, and Rajapaksa thought that the General was trying to upstage him. The disagreement turned into a serious political row as both men became rival candidates in the Presidential elections. It was an election that Rajapaksa would normally be expected to win by a landslide, but Fonseca's rival candidature opened up the prospect of dividing the Singhalese vote and weakening, or even removing Rajapaksa's grip on the country.

The election was fiery to say the least, with a number of murders during the campaign. Incredibly, both candidates tried to reach out to the Tamil population as clearly their votes could make a significant difference. Yet instead of trying to reintegrate a disillusioned group of people, the candidates continued to argue over who should get the credit for winning the war.

Fonseca made a big issue of trying to take the Tamil vote, but only a few months beforehand he had made a big speech in which he had stated that it was clear to him that Sri Lanka was for the Singhalese people and that the Tamils needed to recognise their status as a minority. Imagine the uproar if a US Presidential candidate had said something similar, like the United States is for the Protestant Anglo Saxons and everyone else needs to recognise their status as a minority. Yet Fonseca's speech was not even a discussion point in Sri Lanka. The Singhalese feel that they have the power and there is no question of them sharing it. Not surprisingly, given that both men had been instrumental in the destruction of their entire landscape, the Tamils decided that abstinence was the best course of action and did not vote for either of them. Many political observers felt that the election would be a close call, but in the end it was not as close as some had predicted. Fonseca did make sizeable inroads into the Singhalese vote, but in the end Rajapaksa won with 60 per cent of the total vote.

Unfortunately, the election result was not the end of the feud. On the day of the election, government forces surrounded the General and his staff in the five star Trans Asia hotel in the centre of Colombo in an unexpected and tense standoff. The government forces only backed down after Fonseca's election support staff agreed to leave the hotel and be escorted away from the area by the army. In the days that followed, the General said he would appeal against the election result, which he claimed was rigged, and he accused the President of using state funds to finance his election campaign. He also claimed that the Defence Secretary, the President's brother Gotabaya Rajapaksa, had ordered the killings of surrendering Tamil rebels at the end of the war and he was ready spill the beans in an international court. This coincided with mobile phone video coverage that was circulated at the time that showed a group of Sri Lankan soldiers shooting surrendering Tamils. The clip was even shown on Channel 4 news on British television. Despite independent conformation that the clip is genuine, the Sri Lankan government insist that the video is a fake and that Fonseca is a lying traitor.

Fonseca took a dangerous gamble when he opposed the Rajapaksa family and he is now paying the price. By Presidential decree, he was arrested a few days after the election on the grounds that he was planning to assassinate Rajapaksa and take over the country in a coup d'etat. I expected some kind of street protest from the General's supporters, but apart from a few scuffles, nothing really happened. I do not think that there is any lack of local interest in the Rajapaksa-Fonseca feud. I think that the low key reaction to the news showed one of two things: either a majority of Sri Lankans believed the President and thought that the accusations against the General were true, or more likely in my opinion, that a majority of Sri Lankans were too afraid to publicly denounce the President after seeing the way his government took care of dissenting journalists.

5

I spend much of my time here on my Indian motorbike, a TVS Victor 110 cc, which I drive around in nothing more than shorts, flip-flops and a T-shirt. Driving in Sri Lanka can be great fun, but it can also be incredibly dangerous. It is common, I know, for Westerners to shake their heads at the driving standards they encounter overseas. The generally accepted wisdom is that you need to make allowances for cultural differences, (blah blah), and that you should not judge standards by those you are used to elsewhere. But I do not subscribe to all that. The driving is atrocious so why pretend otherwise? Every day, drivers will drive on the wrong side of the road, run red lights, barge through roundabouts, drive on the pavements, tailgate at high speed or reverse up a main road. People drive either dangerously fast or dangerously slow. They will attempt to pass you on a blind bend up a steep hill. They may stop without warning or they may slow down and then abruptly accelerate if you try and pass them. People ignore lane lines and pass wherever there is a gap, on the inside, outside or quite often by mounting the pavement and scattering pedestrians. Similarly, pedestrians are also unpredictable: they may suddenly decide to cross the road without a glance left or right and step out in front of you, or they may negotiate a fast moving three lane road with a calm stroll across without looking up or breaking stride.

Astonishingly, most of this occurs in front of the police who stand around at all the major junctions and watch impassively. Clearly road anarchy is the accepted norm. No one actually thinks of running a red light as a crime, or that it might be a bit risky to take a call on your motorbike by jamming the phone between your ear and your helmet as you ride along. With all this mayhem on the roads you would expect crashes and carnage everywhere but incredibly accidents are rare. Most cars have scrapes and dents and there is broken glass all over the roads, so evidently, collisions take place. However, it seems that everyone on the road is on the same crazy wavelength following an initially mysterious but mutually understood code of road disorder, and this seems to keep the number of accidents down to a minimum. It is hard to explain, but gradually you begin to unravel the road disorder and intuitively sense when a tuc-tuc in front will stop abruptly with no brake lights and attempt a U-turn, or when a car approaching from the side street will not slow down before swerving onto the main road right in front of you.

One thing that all drivers here have in common is an uncontrollable urge to honk the horn. I can remember coming home in a tuc-tuc from a night out in town and the driver was honking away uncontrollably even though there was no one else on the road. Honking the horn in Sri Lanka is not about warning fellow motorists or pedestrians of your presence. It is more natural reflex; a joyous proclamation of driving without rules and a celebration of reckless abandon. Once you realise this, it becomes infectious. I am now a prodigious honker myself. When the traffic lights turn green, the chorus of honking from everyone eager to rejoin the fray is truly impressive.

I have come to learn that there is a very clear ranking system on the roads in Colombo, like a caste system for vehicles where everyone is expected to know their place. This is inevitable when nobody pays any attention to road signs or normal traffic convention. There has to be some kind of ranking system in the chaos. If a more important, higher ranked vehicle is behind you then it will honk and nudge you until you get out of its way.

Motorbikes, or two wheelers as they are commonly known here, are at the bottom of the pecking order despite the roads being jammed with them. Virtually all of them are cheap and made in India with brands such as TVS, Bajaj and Hero Honda. I paid around 600 dollars for my TVS Victor, which has a top speed of around 35 mph. It sounds a bit like an overheating lawn mower, but I can overtake mopeds and sometimes an overloaded tuc-tuc. Motorbikes swerve in and out of traffic jams at dangerous speeds and in completely random patterns. You often see entire families of four or sometimes five all squeezed on a single motorbike with the smallest child perched on the handlebars and other kids squeezed in between the adults on the seat or on laps. Usually it is only the parents who wear the helmets. Sometimes parents put a wooly hat on young children, and seeing as we are in the tropics and there is no need for extra warmth, it must be as some sort of protection against road rash if they come off. It has to be said, any health and safety inspector worth his salt would never rest in this city.

The tuc-tuc, or Bajaj, or three-wheeler, (sometimes generously referred to as a 'taxi', but usually only by its driver), is a uniquely Asian three-wheeled open sided free spirit of the road. The driver sits on a single seat behind a small windscreen, wiper optional, and steers with a motorbike handle, while he hits the breaks on a floor pedal with his bare feet. Interestingly, bare foot driving is always the preferred option. It is quite common for a driver to remove his shoes and put them down next to the pedals before he sets off. Perhaps it is something to do with having more control when you are able to wrap all your toes around the break pedal. The passengers sit in the back behind an unusual and often ornate silver metal divider, on a sofa seat that holds two comfortably, three with a squeeze, or six or seven if you feel like it, nobody says there is any limit to the number you can try and fit in. Tuc-tucs are everywhere. They stop randomly, drive on pavements, up the wrong side of the road, U-turn suddenly and always pull out slowly in front of speeding traffic. They pester anyone who wants to walk anywhere and they congregate on street corners rather than cruise around like normal taxis so that they can save petrol. Quite often the drivers have a glassy eyed not-quite-with-you look that just adds to the risk of getting a ride in one, but they are so convenient that people get in them all the time. I even took our cat to the vets in one once, but that is something I am not keen to repeat and I still have the scratches to serve as a reminder of her displeasure.

Most of the cars here are nondescript Nissans or Hondas. The import duty on cars shipped into Sri Lanka is enormous and therefore all the cars here are really expensive. When we arrived and I looked into buying a car, I found out that a 10-year-old Honda with 100,000 miles on the clock would cost me around US$15,000, which explains why I have an Indian made motorbike. I still cannot work out how so many Sri Lankans can afford these cars when an average monthly salary is around US$200 a month. There must be some enormous personal debt around (so why don't driving techniques reflect the great expense of the vehicles?)

Moving further up the traffic chain are the Minibuses and 4x4's, often driven by hired drivers with their rich and/or pretentious owners sat in the back. These vehicles are high enough up the chain to not bother too much about what other vehicles are doing. No minibus yields to a tuc-tuc, no 4x4 gives way to a motorbike. These vehicles almost always speed to within a few feet of your back wheel and then lay on the horn until you get out of the way. If I am in a belligerent mood, I hold my ground and let the driver behind honk until he is blue in the face while I tootle along at my own pace taking up the entire lane. This is a dangerous game though, because if one of these vehicles' drivers sense a gap, they will take it and barge past by any means possible, even if it means clipping you as they go past. I know someone who was clipped over on the Galle Road because he did not get out of the way quickly enough. He went sprawling off his moving scooter onto the busy road in a pair of shorts and a T-shirt and no helmet as the guilty driver drove off and nobody stopped to make sure he was okay.

The undisputed king of the road is the Colombo Bus. Belching black smoke and packed with people, these rusty buses thunder and bash their way around the city. The driver has the loudest honker on the road, and he uses it prolifically, as the conductor/tout hangs from the side shouting the destination over and over, in case you missed it the first fifty times. A newspaper article I read said that a recent study had found that 30 per cent of Colombo bus drivers were drug addicts. People were naturally shocked: most thought it was way more than 30 per cent. The buses are truly intimidating as they approach, with the noise and fumes, listing alarmingly through overcrowding and a wrecked suspension; all dents and multicoloured scrapes from the paintwork it has removed from other vehicles. It is crazy to attempt to pass one as it will bear down on you remorselessly. Even trying to pass a stopped bus is risky, as the driver will pull out without a glance as soon as he thinks everyone is onboard. There is also the chance that you will get covered in red gob because many passengers chew paan and spit out the voluminous excess red saliva through the bus window. These grotesque red stains are splattered on all the streets of Colombo. They look like puddles of blood. I have often thought that it would be amusing to go round town with a piece of chalk drawing the outline of a body around the red stain. (I also think it would be amusing to take a marker pen and draw a cock on the forehead of all the posters of Rajapaksa, but in the interests of personal safety, I will not be doing either of these things).

One final note on those buses: I once saw some poor old bloke on a motorbike smash into the back of one because the bus did the unthinkable and paused at a road junction before pulling out. The motorbike rider had assumed the bus would do the usual thing and barge straight out into the road without slowing down, and when it did not the bike had no time left to apply the breaks and he hit the backend of the bus with a splat. See what happens when the code of road disorder is not observed?

6

Mary has started to apply for jobs in the USA and this has cheered me up considerably. I can already detect a softening in my attitude to the various irritants of Colombo now that I have an escape route planned.

However, Mary is a more hesitant about returning home. She says that just because we are moving to a first world country does not mean that we will automatically be rich and that I will never be annoyed by anyone ever again. Of course she is right, but I wish she would not put negative thoughts in my mind. I tend to get carried away with ideas. For example, what if I cannot adapt to the USA? What if no-one will hire me because I am too foreign and then we end up living in a trailer park, shopping with food stamps? Mary and I will succumb to the pressure of having no money and have shouting matches and physical fights that end up on the TV show Cops. (Our faces will be blurred out but everyone will know it's us). I will become enormously fat and ridiculously unkempt and then wear plastic flip-flops and stinky, saggy men's sweat pants to Walmart, where I will shuffle along dragging my shoes on the floor blocking aisles, and when I bend over to get something from the lower shelves, my arse crack will show and someone will take a photo and it will become an internet sensation. Sam will become a big Nascar fan and get a large visible tattoo of a car - and think it is cool - and so get more and more tattoos until his upper torso and legs are completely covered - and then the piercings will start...

Back in the real world, I realise that everything in life carries an element of risk. Even the relatively safe option of finding somewhere nice to settle down and 'be normal'. Clearly I am a changed man, because twenty years ago, settling down somewhere was the last thing I wanted to do. It was the possibility of indiscriminate travel that led me to apply for a job in the Foreign Office. When I got the application papers in the mail there were stories of people in the Foreign Office who had been posted to various, exotic sounding places like Teheran, Paris and Buenos Aires. Right there and then I decided that this was what I wanted to do. I wanted to go to far flung cities. Of course, this was before I became aware of phase three of culture shock and the inherent frustration of living in a third world country. Back then travel was the attraction. The type of work was virtually incidental. I was not drawn to public service, far from it, and to be honest, I do not think I was ever really cut out for diplomatic life. It came as a surprise to most of my family and friends when I landed the job. To be honest, after the job interview, it even came as a surprise to me that I got the job.

My interview, in the summer of 1988, was an unusual affair conducted by three men wearing bow ties and floppy handkerchiefs in their top pockets in an old and elegant room in a building on Whitehall next to Horse Guards Parade. The three of them sat in splendid leather chairs behind an enormous table, in front of a painting of the Battle of Trafalgar and a large framed photograph of the Queen. They all looked as if they had modelled their look on David Niven. I sat in an expensive looking velvet padded armchair, at least twenty feet in front of them, in my one and only suit, bought at Top Shop especially for the occasion, wearing a tie borrowed from my Dad. My look had been modelled on Rick Astley.

The interview was quite bizarre, full of ad hoc general knowledge questions and enquiries about my family and background rather than testing any skills or competences that may have made me suitable for the job. I can remember some of their questions: 'Do you know what NATO stands for?' and 'Who do you think will win the French presidential elections?' and even better, 'Do you know the capital of Outer Mongolia?' and 'What would you do if you had to live there?' I told them that I though that NATO was something to do with the space shuttle and that I had no idea that the French even had elections. However, I did know that Ulan Bator was the capital of Outer Mongolia and I told them I would love to go there. And that seemed to be what the recruiters were looking for: someone crazy enough to go to Outer Mongolia if the Foreign Office posted them there. It was enough for the three David Nivens and I was hired as a junior diplomat.

Looking back it all seemed very easy for me. I always had suspicions that the Foreign Office were under instructions to make their staff more representative of the UK and move away from recruiting from posh schools. Everyone recruited at the same time as me came from Glasgow, Manchester, Newcastle or the East End of London and many new entrants had Asian or Caribbean ancestry, whereas beforehand, it helped if your name was double-barrelled or your dad was a knight of the realm. However, the graduate high flyers, the ones identified as future ambassadors were still picked from the exclusive schools, so when new recruits like me turned up, it created an unusual social mix in the office. People from totally different backgrounds were all thrown together. In my first job, I was the junior clerk in the office along with an East End Londoner, around my age, who came from Ilford. Our boss was a middle aged bloke called Rupert who wore a pinstriped suit to work every day and insisted on calling us both 'my dear chaps'. We were never quite sure if he was speaking in his normal voice or whether he was putting on some camp overly posh accent for our amusement. Rupert was waiting to be appointed as an ambassador somewhere, and was the perfect stereotype of the English gentleman, but instead he got headhunted for another job, as Prince Charles' private secretary, and when he left the Foreign Office he threw a farewell party at some private club in Knightsbridge for the three of us. Like I said, an unusual social mix.

Because I joined the Foreign Office to travel, I found the work was a bit of a distracting nuisance. Also, whenever you were posted overseas, the Foreign Office liked to push the concept that you were always on duty for your country, 24/7, a permanent representative of your country. For example, every few weeks, depending on the size of the embassy, you had to take your turn being the Duty Officer. The DO keeps the contact number that distressed Brits overseas called when they get themselves into trouble, and Britain is such a nation of trouble-makers that the phone used to ring non-stop. The 'representing your country' lark also meant that whenever the ambassador held a function, all the staff were required to attend, to 'work the room' and talk to the distinguished guests. None of the staff could leave until after the last guest had gone and there was no way of slipping out without being noticed. Dinner parties and functions, 'to welcome the trade mission from Crewe', or 'to meet the new ambassador to Greece' used to fill me with dread.

These official functions were made worse for me because I never mastered another language, which meant that conversations were in English or nothing for me. I took some Spanish lessons before going to Montevideo, but it was all a bit half-hearted as I (wrongly) assumed that when I got there, everyone would speak English like they do in Europe. I spent the first year in Montevideo living in ignorance, tuning out of the unintelligible conversations all around me. Getting my hair cut was a potentially disastrous affair. Try going for a haircut with no means of communication with the man with the scissors. It is quite unnerving. In a restaurant, I used to walk round with the waiter and look at other diners' plates, pointing out items of food I wanted: 'Some vegetables like that; one of those steaks over there; some chips like those over here'.

Years later when I was sent to Abidjan in the Ivory Coast and had to learn French, I remembered my Spanish language disaster, but I told myself that I was now more mature and I would make a much bigger effort this time. I went on a six month intensive French course with daily one-on-one lessons with a nice French fellow from Grenoble. I studied hard, listened to French TV and radio and even passed a Foreign Office exam. However, as soon as we got to West Africa I realised quickly that the French I had learnt bore no resemblance to the French spoken by the Ivorians. Ivorian French was unintelligible to me. I spent the entire time in the Ivory Coast bemused, just like in Montevideo.

Luckily, I was not the only non-linguist in the Foreign Office. In Montevideo, a few people from the embassy were having coffee in a café when a friend and colleague of mine asked if anyone knew what the Spanish was for 'milk'. A fairly senior embassy official told my friend that the word was 'leche' and that it was really important that everyone in the embassy learnt and used Spanish properly otherwise it reflected badly on the embassy as a whole. My friend nodded earnestly through all this, and when the waiter came over to our table and poured everyone a black coffee, he seized the moment and said in a broad Liverpool scouse accent, 'Hey mate, can you put some leche in that coffee there please, ta'.

7

It is weeks since the arrest of the General and he is still in jail. Reports emerged that he was unceremoniously dragged from his office by military police, and it was all quite undignified. Still, there has been no major protest. There were some isolated disturbances which allowed the police to fire some tear gas and get the water cannons out, but since then the General has called for calm, (via his wife, as he has no access to the media), and so have some influential Buddhist monks, so the small protests seem to have ended. The police have also arrested the General's son-in-law and seized over half a million US Dollars from the General's relatives. I have no idea what this means, other than they are really going after the Fonseca family. I wonder if the army will rally round their former General or whether they will stay loyal to the President?

When we first arrived in Sri Lanka, the first thing that was really noticeable, apart from the relaxed rules about driving on just the one side of the road, was the huge military presence. Every few yards along the main road from the airport into Colombo there is a soldier pointing his rifle at the traffic. They do not actually do anything as far as I can tell, other than look vaguely menacing and unsettle the few tourists brave enough to come here now on their way to the beaches. There is a military presence at all the major intersections and roundabouts in Colombo, and at key sections of road there are checkpoints where the soldiers pull over vehicles and check ID. Some of the checkpoints are so well established that they have attracted advertising: 'Army Checkpoint — sponsored by Solex Water Pumps — guaranteed for five years!'

Back in 2007 the army presence was understandable, and even reassuring, because terrorism from Tamil Tiger suicide bombers was a regular occurrence. Shortly after arriving in Sri Lanka we travelled to Trincomalee, on the eastern coast of Sri Lanka and until recently part of the Tamil Tiger occupied lands. Trincomalee has a big natural harbour, (the fifth largest in the world according to my guidebook) and the British navy used it in the Second World War to house the ships that fled Singapore when the Japanese invaded. Now the Sri Lankan navy has moved back in after expelling the Tamil Tigers and security in the whole area is intense. In Trincomalee there was a real sense of being close to the front line, something you never really felt in Colombo, even though the military presence in the capital was always high. Instead of standing in the open at the side of the road, soldiers peered out from behind bomb shelters and sand bag bunkers, and instead of berets they wore hard hats and camouflage. Trincomalee is only 250 miles from Colombo but it took us seven hours to get there and ten hours to get back as we passed from one army checkpoint to another. For five Westerners on a minibus, the process involved stopping and getting off the bus while our bags and ID were checked. For those that matched the Tamil Tiger terrorist profile, (which was just about everyone from Trincomalee as it is a predominantly Tamil town) the journey included a body search and your suitcase emptied on the roadside. At each checkpoint there were three or four large old buses with something like 50 or 60 Tamils on board, on their way from the east coast to Colombo. You could see why the checks were so thorough, but after checkpoint number six or seven the sheer inconvenience of it all really begins to bite.

Yet despite all these precautions, the Tamil Tigers still got their bombs through. I lost count of how many went off in our first eighteen months in Sri Lanka. Mostly it was old sari-clad women suicide bombers with explosives taped round them, getting onto a crowded bus, or a government building or a shopping area and setting it all off. Whenever we were on a bus, for example if we were heading to the south coast beaches, any old women who got on alone was always treated with suspicion. Any bag left unattended was an immediate concern. Passengers were incredibly vigilant in scanning for suspicious parcels and bags, and on more than one occasion the news reported incidences of passengers that had saved themselves by identifying a rogue bag and tossing it off the bus before it blew.

In the first six weeks of 2008 alone, shortly after we had arrived in the country, there were twelve large explosions in and around Colombo, and many more in other parts of the country. Hundreds were killed and many more hundreds were injured. Because none of the explosions went off in our part of the city, we were lucky enough not to be in the wrong place at the wrong time. We did not even hear any explosions which made finding out about the events quite a surreal experience. Local TV would often ignore a bombing as a means of delegitimising the work of the Tamil Tigers, so the first we would know about it would be from the BBC on satellite TV. We would recognise the areas of carnage, but still feel detached from it because some newsreader in London was telling us about it. It was no different to watching a report of an explosion in Baghdad. There was no lingering soul-searching or dissection of the event in Sri Lanka, like you would get in England or the United States. People just cleaned up the mess and went about their business again.

Of course, the Sri Lankans had got used to this kind of thing, and I started to agree that it was a good idea to simply get on with life. There was no point in staying at home all the time because you were worried about getting blown up. That said, it is natural to worry about your safety when bombings are so frequent. I knew people who devised contingency escape plans for each of the bars and restaurants they used to visit in case of a bomb.

It was not just individual Tamil Tiger suicide bombers that attacked Colombo. The LTTE also flew two separate night time bombing raids on the city. The Tamil Tigers smuggled a couple of light aircraft into the country in parts, reassembled them in the jungle and then flew south to Colombo to drop bombs from the cockpit. The first attack was over pretty quickly and was fairly quiet. To be honest I had no idea it had even happened until the next morning because it occurred around midnight and I was in bed grumbling about the power cut and how I would have to reset the electric alarm clock.

The second attack was much more dramatic. There was another power cut, this time around 9pm, and almost immediately the night sky was lit up by anti-aircraft fire. I had never witnessed anything like this first-hand before, and it was a real thrill. When you see news footage, of this kind of thing on TV, like Desert Storm air raids, it always appears terrifying, but when confronted with it face-to-face Mary and I were unexpectedly excited. Of course, the huge difference is that in Baghdad the attack usually came from hundreds of modern killer fighter jets, while we were under attack from a reassembled crop sprayer with a single pilot dropping home made bombs off the side. However, this added to the danger. Those US smart bombs hone in on specific targets (most of the time) while our attacker was hoping to hit anything, anywhere.

We took to our roof terrace for a better view, and after a while of marvelling at the brilliant patterns of the red, orange and white anti-aircraft fire, we heard the low buzz of a single light aircraft pass overhead. All around us the zip of hundreds of rounds of tracer fire flew past us, following the plane, and much lower in the sky and closer than they were before. One of the anti-aircraft bullets fizzed past just above our heads and landed on the neighbour's roof. We both knew that the sensible thing to do would be to get inside but we could not draw ourselves away from the light show. All of a sudden an enormous orange glow lit up the horizon in the direction of downtown, followed seconds later by a deafening bang that shook all the windows in the house and toppled ornaments from shelves inside. Clearly there had been a huge explosion in the city. We found out later that the target had been the Sri Lankan navy building, but the pilot had missed and flown kamikaze style into the tax office building nearby, killing 27 people. My mate Rob, the guy a rat snake fell onto when he was lounging by the pool at the Trans Asia hotel, was at the same hotel having dinner with his family, right next to the tax office, when it happened. The hotel staff had moved everyone from the restaurant into the basement for safety and Rob, who is a huge ex-rugby player from the rough end of Liverpool, had to walk round trying to console the terrified tourists who had just arrived in Colombo and were only there for the night before heading off for their beach holiday. The hotel shook to its foundations when the plane crashed and ceilings collapsed and walls and floors cracked dangerously. When everyone got the all-clear, Rob insisted on returning to the restaurant to finish his half eaten steak, despite pleas from the hotel staff not to. Like a good scouser, he wanted his money's worth.

According to the President of Sri Lanka, the War against Terror (he has pinched this line from Bush and Cheney) is now over. The Tamil Tigers have been exterminated and Sri Lanka will go from strength to strength. There is no question that the army have won the war in the north, so why are they still lining the streets, manning the checkpoints and stopping vehicles for ID checks in Colombo? One answer may be that they have nothing else to do. During the war the army set really high levels of recruitment. Chronic over employment is rife here as it is: wander into any shop and there will be five or six assistants following you round asking if you need help. In Sri Lanka, words like potato peeler, dishwasher, coffee maker and fly swatter do not refer to household items, they are job titles. Now that there is no one left to fight, what else can these soldiers do other than man their checkpoints and keep their roadside sentry? Sometimes I wonder whether enough of them will be tempted to spring the General from prison, just for something to do. Then again, as long as the General maintains that he is willing to testify about war crimes being committed then a lot of soldiers might think it is better if their former boss was kept quiet and locked up.

8

When we lived in Abidjan, in the Ivory Coast, I was still working for the Foreign Office, and contrary to what the Daily Mail will tell you, we did not live in a mansion at taxpayers' expense (although we did have a swimming pool, ha!). Abidjan is not the capital of the Ivory Coast, or Cote d'Ivoire as we got used to calling it because that is what they call it there, being all French speakers. The capital is a place called Yamoussoukro, which is over a hundred and fifty miles away in the middle of the jungle. The Ivorian government was always asking embassies to move their mission to the capital, but not surprisingly, everyone always came up with reasons why we should stay put. Abidjan is a big and vibrant city: ten times bigger than Yamoussoukro, and far more economically important. In fact, I remember being quite surprised by the size of the city when I first arrived, especially as I had hardly heard of the place beforehand. For example, did you know that Abidjan is the fourth biggest French speaking city in the world, after Montreal, Paris and Kinshasa? It is. I think that is pretty impressive.

On my first trip into Abidjan from the airport (named after the first president with the improbable name of Felix Houphouet-Boigny) I remember being taken aback by the long smooth,

French style wide boulevards through busy commercial districts called Treichville and Zone Quatre. I seem to recall that I wondered whether I had underestimated Cote d'Ivoire. After forty minutes you get your first glimpse of downtown, called Le Plateau, with its built up towers situated around a lagoon and reached by a long bridge. With only a moderate sized amount of imagination, you could be heading towards Manhattan. It is only when you got up close to the tall apartment and business tower blocks that you see the concrete falling away and the rusted metal. Nonetheless, Abidjan looked like a proper city, superficially at least. In the Sixties, Abidjan was sometimes called the 'Paris of Africa', and when we were there you could still see why. Funnily enough, the legend of the origin of the name 'Abidjan' always made me smile. When the first French colonists asked native women the name of the place by the lagoon, they replied 'T'chan m'bidjan' which apparently means, 'Eh? I've just been cutting trees'.

Abidjan was the only other place we lived where the army had a profile as high as it is in Sri Lanka. We moved there in April 2000, just a few months after a military coup had removed the democratically elected President. The new man in charge of the country was a tough Army leader with an uncompromising attitude and an amusingly camp name, General Guei (pronounced Gay).

Just like in Colombo, there were army checkpoints everywhere. People were stopped and harassed and you always needed to justify where you were going and why. Tanks sat on street corners and armed guards sped round the city on the back of army motorbikes. Yet in contrast with Sri Lanka these days, we never found ourselves wondering why there was such a high level of security. Rebel groups in the north of the country wanted to seize power and they started a bloody battle with the Army to try and seize control themselves. The streets were not safe to wander around and the embassy provided day and night guards to protect us. Although, in truth, I am not sure how much protection a barefoot, unarmed, sleeping guard would have provided. They would turn up for work hungry, so we fed them each day. We also tried to converse but they all came from Burkina Faso (the new name for Upper Volta) and they spoke French with an accent quite unintelligible to my hastily European French trained ear.

Fighting used to break out indiscriminately all over the city. One of the guards turned up late for work one morning and when I asked him why, he showed me his bruises and told me that he had been beaten up for being from Burkina Faso. On another morning, on my way to work, I reached a large junction that was normally full of cars, but for some reason that morning was quiet. Pedestrians on my right hand side suddenly started to run and scream and gunshots rang out overhead, echoing off the buildings. I was less than a mile from the embassy so I thought I would make a dash for there. I pulled out quickly into the junction and on my right side saw an army gunman walk out into the street and point his rifle at my car. He lifted the rifle slightly and sent a round of gunfire straight over the roof of my car. If he wanted to send me a signal to get off the streets he could not have been clearer. I raced to the office, where the embassy guard made me stop, reverse back up the car park ramp and wind down the window so he could tell me he thought he had heard gunfire so I had better get inside. After a quick grunt and growl, I went to the roof to watch smoke rising in flumes across the city and gunshots randomly ring out in the first of what was many revolts in the city.

I was joined shortly by Debbie, a friend and colleague, and her husband Stewart who worked for Reuters. Stew had been driving Debbie into work when two army officers jumped in front of Stew's car and waved him down to stop. They told them that they needed to immediately commandeer the vehicle and asked Stew for his mobile telephone number so they could return the car when they had finished. Stewart and Debbie did not hold out much hope of getting the car back, seeing as the

Army were clearly planning on using it during the conflict. And yet, one week later, Stew got a call from the Army thanking him for his assistance and they arranged to return the car with a full tank and a pile of spent rifle shells on the back seat.

This kind of revolt became so common over the next year that they became part of life. It is quite awful to admit, but, while people were being killed in the street a few miles from my house in a political and religious battle for the country, I was often lying by our pool drinking gin and tonic. I was always aware of what was happening because all staff had been issued with (no expense spared) huge, brick shaped short circuit radios. They were not secure at all and anything we said could have been picked up with a simple radio, so we all had cunning call signs based on a bird theme to confuse the enemy. As with everything in the Foreign Office, recognising the hierarchy was paramount. Therefore, the Ambassador needed something majestic and so he was called 'Eagle'. The more junior staff like me had names like 'Sparrow' and 'Blackbird'. The office messenger was called 'Pigeon', and the office tarts were 'Thrush' and 'Swallow'. Ingenious.

My friend Tommy ('Blue Tit') lived near the television studios which became a key battle ground as rival groups fought over the right to broadcast their propaganda. He used to calmly report over the radio in his broad Glaswegian accent the events that were occurring right next to his house. I remember him describing a stampede: 'I can hear the sound of a thousand flip-flops running past ma hoose!' and a drinking competition with a difference when he and another colleague saw how long they could sit outside on the patio with their 'Flag' beers before the tear gas cloud that wafted over from the battleground forced them to go back inside.

Tommy was in charge of the visa section in the embassy, and part of my job required me to cover his leave absences, even though I knew nothing about the visa application process. Because the country was in such a mess, there were always large queues of people looking to get to the UK any way they could. Forged bank statements were very common, as were forged letters of recommendation or forged letters with job offers. One morning I was helping Tommy in the visa section when a young Ivorian popped up at the window and handed over a letter from Arsenal football club offering him a trial. Tommy was instantly suspicious, having had a number of Ivorians with similar letters over the last couple of weeks. He asked a few questions and looked at the letter, which appeared genuine, stamped with a big embossed Arsenal letterhead and signed by the Arsenal Chief Scout. Tommy looked at me, then at the applicant, then back at me and smiled. He disappeared off to a back room and returned holding a football.

'Right' he said. 'If you're going to play for the Arsenal, then you'll be able to do a few keepy-uppys with the ball, won't you?'

He threw the ball over the counter and the young applicant instantly began heading the ball up and bouncing it on his knee, shoulder, back of the neck, inside of foot and outside of foot. There must have been close to a hundred people crowded into the little visa section waiting room and they all gathered in a circle round the young star cheering and clapping. After a brilliant five minute show, Tommy shouted his approval and told the young guy that he could have his visa. The young Ivorian handed over his passport and we noted his name, thinking he was a star of the future, and we turned out to be right. It was Kolo Toure, who went on to captain Arsenal and the Ivory Coast.

Although most of the violence took place a few miles from our house, we did have one close encounter. I woke up around 3am one night to hear shouting and what sounded like gun shots from the house next door. Mary had slept through it all so I did wonder whether I had imagined it, but to be on the safe side I thought I would peer out the side window next to the front door and see whether the guards looked as if they had heard anything suspicious. I realised that something must be happening because both guards looked alert, rather than lying flat out asleep on the driveway on a piece of cardboard. When one of the guards saw me he explained (with much miming so I could understand him) that there had been a robbery at the house next door and that some shots had been heard. As my guards were armed with nothing more than a torch and a whistle and they were worried that the burglar was still loose in the area, they had pressed the big, bright red 'ONLY USE IN EMERGENCIES' super emergency button that calls for the security company rapid response SWAT team.

I thought that I had better stay awake until the swat team arrived as they would probably want to speak to me and I also wanted to see the super SWAT team in action with my own eyes, so I made myself a cup of tea and went to sit in the living room which looked out onto the back garden through huge floor to ceiling windows. As the back garden was surrounded by high walls and was usually quiet we had no nets or curtains, so when my two security guards and a white guy with a gun wearing an officious looking uniform with 'Securicor' on the back appeared, they all saw me through the window, sitting in my underpants drinking my cup of tea.

I realised the white guy must be a South African because 'Securicor' was a South African company. I also realised quickly that he was the only member of the 'rapid response swat team', which shattered my apparently delusional expectations of a crack team of guards all rushing to our aid. I thought I would go outside and ask him what had happened in English to make sure I had understood the French-speaking guard correctly. I went out into the garden (in my underpants, carrying my tea, what the hell) and stood there good humouredly taking in the scene of a man dressed like Rambo pointing his torch and his gun round my back garden like they do in American movies. I was pretty certain that no one was back there as I had been sitting having my tea for ten minutes and would have noticed someone creeping around the garden. I was just about to open my mouth to say something to the South African when he spun round with his revolver, pointed at something in the darkness, shouted 'Over there!' and shot his pistol three times into the garden.

I do not know what was more alarming: standing so close to a smoking revolver, with a deafening ringing in my ears, and a pumped up and sweating South African looking for something else to shoot, or the fact that there may be a dead burglar back there prostrate in the bushes next to my patio furniture, BBQ and umbrella. Before I could catch my breath, one of the night guards shouted in French that something moved to the right, so the South African fired off three more rounds into the darkness. This time a cat bounded across the lawn at a breakneck speed away from the danger zone.

When everyone calmed down, a quick inspection revealed that it had been the face of the wooden mask, which we had fitted to a tree, (the same mask that now has the wasp nest!) that had drawn the first round of shots, and the movement of the cat that had drawn the second. It is hard to describe the relief you feel when you discover that you do not, after all, have a bullet riddled African thief in your back garden. The wooden mask was not hit either, but there were three nice big bullet holes in the tree underneath it. I gave a hesitant thanks to the South African and went back to bed, where Mary was still fast asleep, unaware of the night drama. Of course, I shook her awake and told her everything. News like that cannot wait until the morning.

It turned out that the burglar from next door did not jump into my garden, which undoubtedly prevented him from being shot, but he still suffered an undignified end. My Ivorian neighbour had been the one who fired the first shots that started the whole drama and he had given chase as soon as he realised that he had been broken into. He chased the intruder onto a patch of wasteland behind his house where he discovered a half hidden bag full of things stolen from his house. Rather than take the bag and count his blessings that nothing had been lost and no-one had been hurt, my neighbour left the bag where it was and lay in wait in camouflage until the burglar returned to collect his stolen goods. He then jumped the burglar, punched him senseless and called the police to come and collect him. He was waiting for the police, sitting on the burglar in the street while pointing a gun to his head as I left for work the next morning. He gave me a nonchalant wave as if he did this kind of thing all the time.

9

There are long standing and close ties between Sri Lanka and Britain but in recent times they have begun to unravel. There were even a couple of demonstrations outside the British High Commission in response to Rajapaksa speeches about British interference in his country, and at one point someone had amusingly daubed 'Tamil Tiger HQ' on the wall. (Incidentally, the High Commission is called that, and not an embassy, because Sri Lanka is in the Commonwealth. All members of the Commonwealth call their mission a High Commission in other member countries. A mission in a non-Commonwealth country is called an embassy. For example, Britain has an embassy in Paris and in Washington, but it has a High Commission in India and Australia. To complete the etiquette, a mission in a city that is not the capital, for example, the British mission in New York City, is called a Consulate-General. It is all unnecessarily complicated if you ask me, and I used to be paid to know this kind of thing).

Sri Lanka's relationship with many other Western countries has become similarly strained. The US made some remarks about about human rights abuses and in response the Sri Lankan Prime Minister, Ratnasiri Wickremanayake, made the inappropriate though amusing comment on Sri Lankan radio that Hillary Clinton had forgotten the 'Monica Lewinsky episode' and needed to 'put her house in order'. The Sri Lankans also started a war of words with the United Nations. When the UN announced they would set up a panel to advise the Secretary General on Sri Lanka's human rights accountability, the Sri Lankan Foreign Minister, GL Peiris, stormed that Sri Lanka was now fed up with these calls to look into war crimes. He argued that Sri Lanka was being 'harassed' and that any UN inquiry in war crimes would be flawed and unfair, seeing as all the Tamil Tigers leadership has been killed and the Government side will get all the blame. I think, Mr. Peiris, that is the point of the enquiry.

Amnesty International has waded into the argument and has criticised the United Nations over their non-intervention during the end of the civil war in Sri Lanka. Above all, Amnesty are outraged that power plays at the UN meant that member states approved a resolution drafted by Sri Lanka that complimented itself on its success against the Tamil Tigers. The secretary general of Amnesty, Claudio Cordone, told the BBC that 'one would be hard pressed to imagine a more complete failure to hold to account those who abused human rights'.

Sri Lanka has also clashed with the EU. After repeated warnings the European Union suspended Sri Lanka's preferential trade benefits because of concerns over the country's human rights record. There are large numbers of clothes factories here that make cheap clothes for big retailers like Next and M&S, and losing the preferential trade benefits will probably mean that the factories move to cheaper neighbouring competitors. Sri Lanka would lose money and jobs. But it looks as though Rajapaksa is happy to accept that rather than answer meddlesome questions about human rights. Especially now that he has made some new, more powerful friends.

China has rapidly become Sri Lanka's number one benefactor and it was Chinese hardware that gave the Sri Lankan army the weaponry that helped them end the stalemate in the long war. In return, China has been granted a series of big infrastructure projects in Sri Lanka, such as the funding of a large coal power station, the construction of a network of new roads and railways, the construction of a huge performing arts hall in Colombo and the building of a brand new international airport in the south of the island. But the biggest project of them all is the development of a new seaport at Hambantota on the south coast. The first phase, which is due to be completed in August, will be for commercial traffic. It is a move that Rajapaksa has said will put Sri Lanka 'on the path to being the true Wonder of Asia'. But it is the second phase that has generated interest from most observers and it appears to be the main reason for China's new found investment programme in Sri Lanka. The port is due for a huge expansion, and it looks as though the expansion will be purely for the benefit of the Chinese navy. This has certainly concerned India, traditionally Sri Lanka's main influence and benefactor, and they see it as another clear sign that the Chinese are stepping up their influence in the Indian Ocean.

Diplomatic relations between Sri Lanka and the UK deteriorated further after the British foreign secretary and prime minister both spoke at a conference in London organised by a group called the Global Tamil Forum. The Sri Lankan government considered the conference a pro-LTTE event even though the organiser, a man named Father Emmanuel, a 75 year old Catholic priest, set up the conference based on the principles of democracy and non-violence in the spirit of the 'principles of emancipation promoted by Mahatma Gandi, Nelson Mandela and Martin Luther King'. It does not sound like a militant terrorist group to me.

At the conference, David Milliband, the foreign secretary, repeated calls for an investigation into allegations that both the Sri Lankan state and the Tamil Tigers violated international humanitarian law during last year's fighting. Maybe Milliband should think about having MI6 agents spring General Fonseka from jail. Apparently he knows all about the abuses that went on.

Incidentally, everyone in Sri Lanka refers to the Tamil Tigers as the LTTE. The name 'Tamil Tigers' appears to be used only by the Western media as far as I can tell. No one here calls them anything other than LTTE. Maybe it is down to the fondness for acronyms and use of initials. To give just one everyday example, people do not send a text message here, they send an SMS. Acronyms are entrenched in politics, with party names such as the UNP, SLFP, JVP, ULF, PA, UPFA and JHU. Revered former leaders are referred to using their initials, like DS Senanayake and SWRD Bandaranaike. The only time that I saw that an acronym had not been used was when I saw a billboard advertising a conference of the Sri Lankan Union of Teachers, but given that the acronym for them would be 'SLUT', I think someone must have had a word and asked them to drop it.

10

It gets so hot in Colombo that you can boil an egg on the roof terrace and the humidity is so high that I regularly need to change my sopping shirt and underpants two or three times a day. This is no exaggeration. It is quite incredible. We have three ceiling fans in the house: one in each bedroom and one in the lounge, but I rarely turn the one in the lounge on as it is so noisy that you cannot hear the TV and the ceiling is so low that the fan just misses my head when I stand up. Consequently, the lounge is like a sweat-lodge. In the bedrooms we do have old noisy air conditioners along with the fans, but we cannot have them on for more than ten minutes before we go to bed because the cost of running them is astronomical. Our last electricity bill was for over three hundred pounds, and we spend most of the time sitting in hot darkness. It is 33 degrees centigrade and 100 per cent humidity both at midday and at midnight, and the only breeze we have is furnace hot. Everyone keeps commenting on how hot it is at the moment, like it is something out of the ordinary. But to me it is always this hot. The only thing that changes is the amount of rain that falls. It is either very hot and very sunny or very hot and very cloudy and wet. The tropics zap your strength, energy and optimism. All I can do is lie around in a heat induced lethargy. I notice that even our cat, Poppy, regularly cannot summon the energy to move. I once saw her ignore a lizard that walked brazenly past her outstretched paw. The heat builds up incrementally from January to May when the monsoon finally comes and cracks the stifling air with loud, vibrant, electric thunderstorms and torrential rainstorms.

The heat and rain and humidity has created huge fungus patches on our ceiling and walls and the bathroom is all mold and mildew, despite getting pretty regular and severe dettol wash downs. Unfortunately, the fungus seems to have transferred to us too and we regularly suffer from nasty boils and heat induced rashes, particularly around our more sensitive regions. Mary went to see the doctor about this and was prescribed some cream for the problem area. When she went to the pharmacist to collect the cream the young chemist behind the counter insisted on saying loudly in front of all the other customers that the cream was for the vagina:

'Do not be using this cream on any area except the vagina, Madam' he said while pointing to her crotch. 'This cream is only for rubbing on the vagina, Madam. Only on the vagina'.

Spending so much time overseas invariably means that you come face to face with previously unknown and nasty diseases. On one occasion when we lived in Kenya, Mary and I both came out in nasty red rashes over our face, neck, arms and legs that looked just like peeled away skin leaving behind a red mark that looked tender and sore, like a severe burn. However, they were completely painless and we did not even know we had them until we recognised them on each other with lots of horrified screaming and pointing. We went straight to the doctor who unnervingly admitted to us that he was completely mystified. He had seen nothing like it and could not work out what had caused the painless burn marks. As we felt fine, we were sent home with nothing more than some soothing cream. Over the next few days, we noticed that other people had contracted the same thing. People all over Nairobi were walking around with huge, disfiguring red sores all over their bodies, particularly on the face. It transpired that the burns were down to a small fly that had descended upon the city. As people brushed them away, the fly left behind a small amount of acid that burned the skin and left the horrible red marks, but somehow the burns were administered painlessly. It became known locally as 'Nairobi eye' because most of the burn marks occurred around that area of the face. It seemed to effect just about everyone. Everyone at work was disfigured for a week. The Ambassador made a big speech to a bunch of visiting British industrialists with red burns all over his nose. Even President Moi of Kenya appeared on television with red flaps of burnt skin around his eyes. No one was immune. And then, just as suddenly as they had appeared, the fly was gone and 'Nairobi eye' became a thing of the past, no harm done.

11

Sam and I always walk to school in the morning, which is my favourite part of the day because I love walking and it is generally as cool as it is ever going to get at 7am. We walk past a Buddhist temple, along railway tracks, down the side of the golf course, (past 'I'll get it') and then along a narrow road, which is always teeming with life and activity, until we reach the school gates. The whole walk takes about 15 minutes, and we always see the same characters. Sam, with his blonde hair, is a magnet for attention, and it has taken him three years to get used to people touching his hair, or kissing his hand. On one memorable occasion, an old woman came rushing out of the house to kiss him on the cheek. Forever after he warily crossed the road when we approached her house.

At the end of our little street is a small Buddhist temple where the boss monk stands outside in his crimson gown, nodding his shaved head at passers-by. I had this impression that Buddhist monks would be serene beings, constantly on the verge of nirvana and at peace with the world. This one does not fit my pre-conceived image, however, as instead of nodding a greeting in the morning he gives me a long hard stare, quite often when he is chatting on his mobile phone. It is not an aggressive stare, but I find it quite uncomfortable to be stared out by a monk. Possibly, he can detect bad vibes or something else spiritually amiss about me, but I suspect there are other forces at work. According to Mary, the monk gives her a very jolly wave and smiles every morning. He obviously likes the look of her chakras.

Past the temple is where the tuc-tuc drivers park and hang around for fares. There are around four or five drivers here at any one time, which is extremely convenient for getting about town on those days when you would rather someone else tackled the traffic mayhem for you. All sorts of local characters hang around with the drivers. There is the one-eyed man who wanders about in a permanent daze; the man in the tatty sarong who sweeps up all the leaves and burns them with much gusto in the street; the government worker who walks round with his large pole with the hook to reach up and switch off the manual switches of the street lamps; the small, fat 'toad-man' who sits on his small chair/toadstool and waves at everyone; the jolly postman in tatty shorts and a t-shirt on his pushbike; and the neighbourhood drunk who sits on a wall wearing a Sri Lanka one-day international cricket shirt, clutching a bottle of local moonshine called kassippu, shouting indiscriminate insults at people who pass by. I used to try and give the drunk a wide berth, but recently we seem to have struck up an understanding. Actually, perhaps an understanding would be overstating it, as the only word I can pick out of his mutterings is 'darling', which makes me wonder what his intentions are.

I have actually been approached twice, quite openly and brazenly, by homosexuals in Sri Lanka. I am not sure whether this is something to be proud of, or something to be concerned about. The first time was when Mary, Sam and I were walking along the beach in Unawatuna, a lovely beach village near Galle in the south of Sri Lanka. A boy of around sixteen or maybe even younger came up to me and started smiling: nothing unusual there, so I smiled back. After the briefest of introductions, and just enough time for Mary and Sam to walk out of earshot, he let it be known that he liked men, and he liked me and could we go for a walk together somewhere quiet to 'get to know each other a bit better'. I was too shocked to say anything so ended up running away, looking repeatedly over my shoulder, grimacing and shaking my head. You have to wonder about the type of people who visit Unawatuna if that sort of approach has worked for him in the past. Of course, it rapidly dawned on me that I must have matched this kid's profile of a married man on the look out for a bit of young boy on the side, which is an uncomfortable realisation, to put it mildly.

The second approach happened a couple of weeks ago outside one of the supermarkets in Colombo. The supermarket has introduced this ludicrous system of taking a ticket at the car park entrance, redeeming it in the supermarket at a special counter and then handing it in at a specially constructed exit, even though the supermarket is out of town and the car park is always empty. Still, it keeps around six people employed, which is perhaps the whole point. It was one of the car park attendants who approached me. He said he liked the look of my face and wanted my mobile number as he would like me to be his boyfriend. I blustered that I did not have a mobile phone, much to the amusement of the tuc-tuc driver, who was one of the regular drivers from the end of the street. I am sure the tuc-tuc driver took great delight in re-telling this little episode to the rest of his mates on the corner. Nobody has mentioned the episode to me directly but I have noticed sniggering when I have walked by recently. Come to think of it, it seems to have coincided with the drunk guy calling me his 'darling'.

Just past the tuc-tuc corner is the railway crossing, where, in contrast to such places in most parts of the world, people gather and engage in all sorts of activity despite the regular close shave transit of huge, noisy, black smoke belching trains. A whole gang of men live on the tracks and make a living by recycling garbage. When they are not rifling through rubbish bags or pinching the flowers left by the graves in the nearby cemetery, they are usually to be seen smoking opium. Nalinika, my neighbour, has warned me about speaking to 'those drug addicts', but I have found them a friendly bunch. They always smile and say good morning, apart from when they have scored some heroin, and then they squat or lie down flat on the ground and gaze off into the distance. At first I could not understand how on some mornings these men would be so friendly, and then on other occasions they would completely ignore me. I thought they were all bipolar until I realised that they were not smoking Dunhill's or Marlboro Lights. One of the tuc-tuc drivers told me that the heroin they smoked came from Pakistan and sold for just under a dollar for a cigarette. I can sort of understand why they do it. They have a very hard and a mostly shit life. If they can get some release for less than a dollar, then why not? I probably indirectly fund some of this drug abuse in any case because I give them all my empty bottles so they can take them to the corner shop and get cash refund on the glass.

We have to walk for some metres along the railways tracks to reach the golf course, and more than once we have had to run for safety because of an oncoming train. This is not as scary or perilous as it sounds because the trains move so slowly I reckon Sam and I could actually outrun one if we had to. There is a man who controls a rail crossing alarm and a barrier where the tracks cross the street where the recycling heroin addicts live, but he seems to be a forgetful character judging by the number of times he does not lower the barriers at all. On these occasions, the first anyone knows about the oncoming train is when it comes round the corner of the track blowing its horn. I have watched the barrier man on many occasions leisurely stroll to his little room with the control and drop the barrier just a couple of seconds before the train rumbles past. It is almost not worth the effort. People tend to hear the train way ahead in any case, and no vehicle crosses the tracks without slowing to a stop and looking to see themselves if there is anything coming.

Word gets around and everyone knows that the barrier man is a liability. The whole road crossing is fairly amateur in any case, as the alarm is a little bell pulled with a bit of string and one of the two wooden barriers has been snapped in half. The recyclers and anyone else on the tracks tend to carry on with their business until the train is almost upon them, and vehicles manoeuvre around the barriers to cross the tracks if their friends standing on the tracks tell them that the coast is clear.

The golf course path is full of shade and wildlife: the cobra, of course, but many other snakes too, as well as dozens of huge water monitor lizards and pelicans and kingfishers. The golf course guards smile and say good morning as we walk nonchalantly past the huge golf course sign warning that the golf course is private property, that all trespassers will be prosecuted, and rather more bizarrely, that absolutely no grazing of livestock is allowed on the fairway.

The final part of our walk is along a narrow street, with small shacks on one side, occupied by women cleaning and sweeping and cooking, and shady trees on the other, where their men sit on chairs and watch them. The shacks are identical, lined up like a terrace, with one small door and no window and a corrugated metal roof. The door is always left wide open to let in some air for the sometimes five or six people who sit around sharing the single room. Cockerels run around, water monitor lizards scurry across the path and stray dogs wander in and out of homes. In the morning, we pass people with huge mouthfuls of toothpaste, because the shacks do not have indoor plumbing water and so people brush their teeth in the street and take water from small communal taps by the side of the road. We also pass a communal well, where people bathe happily in sarongs by the side of the road next to passersby by pouring bucketfuls of water repeatedly over their heads.

We often speak to some of the characters that live in this street, and Sam appears to be some sort of mini-celebrity as far as they are concerned. Most of the men refer to him as 'young master' or 'baby Beckham' because he often takes his football to school and they like to pat him on the head as we walk past. One of these characters told me that he used to play football for Sri Lanka and as if to prove his football credentials, often stands around in a full Arsenal replica strip including football boots, despite being well into his forties. He introduced himself as 'Semen', which of course made me wary of his intentions, and when I asked him to repeat his name, thinking I must have misunderstood him, he repeated again that he was called 'Semen'.

Not wanting to acknowledge the obvious name association, I found myself floundering and talked myself into trouble, 'Ah, semen, like, as in, ... erm ....'

'You know why!' he proclaimed loudly. 'I am named after the great goalkeeper for Arsenal, Mr. David Seaman'.

Another man who lives somewhere near the narrow street, but not in one of the shacks as far as I can work out, usually makes a special effort to come and have a few words each morning with me. It is hard to fathom his exact age because he is so weathered and worn. I think he lives permanently outside, and he could be anything from fifty to seventy depending on how long he has been living rough. He wears the same sarong and battered t-shirt with 'Hot Stuff' on the front every day and smiles a big toothless grin. We often see him by the heroin smokers, walking around the tracks in his bare feet, picking carefully over the broken glass and sharp stones. One day, he asked me what I did for a living and he gave me the strangest look of incredulity when I told him I did not work. He informed me proudly that he worked with Greenpeace and had done so for many years. I looked at him again, and thought I must have misunderstood. I am an open minded kind of guy, but I could not for the life of me see this man in the forefront of the fight against climate change, the protection of the oceans and the movement for nuclear disarmament. It crossed my mind, presumptuously, that maybe he was a driver or gardener at the Greenpeace office, but he insisted that he was the big man in Colombo in Greenpeace. He said that if I asked anyone in the area they would tell me that he was 'Mr. Greenpeace'. He promised to fetch me his business card the next day, which he did, and it proudly announced his name with the catchy slogan, 'Mr Green Peas: green peas grown and delivered to your door!'

12

Getting into a tuc-tuc with a driver you know is much easier than flagging one down on the street and negotiating a price. I have arranged mutually agreed fares with the drivers at the end of the street for most trips into town, but getting a driver you do not know for the return trip is much more problematic and involves a long negotiation over the price beforehand.

You also need to be acquainted with Sri Lankan head wobbling. A wobble is not to be confused with a head shake, because a wobble usually means that some sort of agreement has been reached. The level of head wobbling can range from an almost imperceptible twitch to full on sideways jiggling, depending on the depth of agreement reached. It took me months to work all this out. Negotiating a fare when you are not sure whether you are getting a wobble or a shake can be very tricky.

When the price has been agreed you still have to worry about the man behind the wheel and whether he is capable of getting you home in one piece. I once jumped into the back of a tuc-tuc and wondered vaguely if I had been driven by that particular driver before because for some reason he looked somewhat familiar. Then, he as floored the accelerator, pulled out in front of a speeding bus and started zigzagging through the traffic at an alarming pace, I suddenly remember that I recognised him because the last time I had a ride in his tuc-tuc he scared the living shit out of me. I think my Colombo guidebook suggests that in moments like this it is advisable to ask the driver to stop and look for a different ride home. The reality is that it is just far easier to hang on and hope for the best. I do not want to be dumped on the side of the road in a strange part of town in the beating sun while the rejected driver negotiates an inflated fee for the distance travelled to that point.

Most tuc-tuc drivers like to talk to foreigners, and incredibly almost every conversation follows the same pattern. Perhaps all tuc-tuc drivers buy the same conversational English book. The essential opening line is: 'You are from?' usually accompanied by nods of approval if you reply England (it is down to cricket, not the political legacy or the railways and the excitement is usually a result of the stack of additional cricket questions forming in the driver's head). After the opening there is always a question about Sri Lanka, and whether you like it here. Of course, I always say that I do, although I usually roll my eyes at the same time if they are not looking. The final question is always about employment: who do I work for and what do I do in Sri Lanka. I get some fairly astonished looks when I tell them that my wife works and I stay at home and clean and cook. Sometimes this revelation is so shocking that it completely kills the conversation. I do not even get the additional cricket questions and the driver resorts to giving me funny looks in the rear view mirror.

Many people will tell you that Sri Lanka is home to the friendliest people on earth, and it is true that people are generally quick to smile here and it is an endearing trait. Walk down any street and people will be quick to greet you and ask you how you are. Yet, it appears to me that Sri Lankans are very quick to judge each other, to categorise each other, and to establish a social strata.

The caste system is not as deeply engrained as the Indian version, but it is still alive inside Sri Lankan minds. The Singhalese divide themselves into the Kandyans and the low country or Southern castes, and the Tamils divide themselves into Northern and Eastern castes. Different castes align themselves with different occupations: for example, the Singhalese low country traditional land workers would come from the Govigama caste. However, quite clearly, caste is not the most important identifier in Sri Lanka: it is ethnicity and religion. Singhalese, Buddhist, Tamil, Hindu, Muslim and Christian are far more important badges than traditional occupation.

Unquestionably, the Buddhists rule Sri Lanka and they see it as their promised land. It is not dissimilar to the way that Jews see Israel as their promised land. Other religions are tolerated in Sri Lanka: the Tamils are Hindu, and there are significant Muslim and Christian populations. But I do not think anyone is in any doubt where the power lies: the Sinhalese Buddhists. Sometimes the Buddhist superiority complex can appear bizarrely paranoid. For example, in early 2010 a Sri Lankan woman, Sarah Malanie Perera, who had converted to Islam after living for some years in Bahrain, was arrested in Colombo for having a Singhalese name but wearing the clothes and acting in the manner of Muslim woman.

I am asked all the time if I am a Christian. It is a vital part of identity here, and it is needed to properly determine your standing in society. At first I used to tell anyone that asked that I was an Atheist, that I was not a Christian because I did not believe in all that ritualistic nonsense. But the shock and confusion this caused made me change tactic pretty quickly. To avoid a prolonged discussion about it, I now always tell people that I am indeed a Christian. If I am in the mood, I put on a serious and earnest look and tell people that I am a reborn evangelistic holy and devoted follower of the baby Jesus. Nobody has yet detected the sarcasm.

CULTURE SHOCK AND TIGER BOMBS

Without question, I am a difficult one for many of our Sri Lankan neighbours to categorise properly in their social ladder. I am not even a typical foreigner as I do not own a car and I am not a member of any clubs and I do not even work. I chat to the tuc tuc drivers and the railway track heroin addicts as much as I chat to my rich Sri Lankan neighbours, and more importantly, I speak to them politely and with respect. It is this particular aspect that seems to be major point of difference, because I have seen some quite outrageous behaviour by rich Sri Lankans towards those who they consider below them on the social ladder. I have seen golfers kick their caddies in disgust after a bad shot and on hot days, these same golfers get their caddies to trail after them holding an umbrella for shade from the sun and then scold them if they do not keep up. I have seen waiters patronised, pinched and prodded by rich men in restaurants. I have seen drivers scolded and slapped by rich women in car parks. At the school, I have seen mothers call for house staff to fetch them chairs to sit on, and then not acknowledge them with any gratitude when they struggle back carrying a chair. The same applies if you hold a door open for certain Sri Lankans following you out of an office or shop, which I think is basic good manners, but usually goes without acknowledgement or thanks here. Because of this I have started slamming doors behind me now, trying to time it perfectly so that the person behind is inconvenienced to the maximum.

This Sri Lankan social hierarchical behaviour is most evident to me at the supermarket when the rich Sri Lankan women make one of their rare excursions from the home. (The supermarkets, incidentally, are all designed so that the aisles are too narrow for two trolleys to pass, so everyone needs to push and squeeze uncomfortably past each other in the aisles. I think it is all part of a more general cultural acceptance of closeness. Personally, I find it an invasion of personal space). Rich women do not push supermarket trolleys themselves; they get their drivers to do it for them. They also get their driver to pick up the groceries from the shelves, put them in the trolley and bag up the vegetables. At the checkout counter, the checkout girl removes everything from the trolley, rings up the bill and then puts everything in a bag and the Madam stands there, watching all this impassively without lifting a finger to help. The driver rushes outside to move the 4x4 right outside the exit and then jumps out of the car to put the groceries inside. I assume that when they get home, the housemaid will unpack everything and then cook it. And all of this is done under the critical glare of the Madam, and if anything is not done to her satisfaction, the poor driver, or checkout girl, or housemaid will get scalded or slapped. I know what you are thinking: what a generalisation; not all rich Sri Lankan women carry on in this way. Well, no of course not. I am generalising, not everyone is the same. But like all stereotypes, it is a general trait and I would not have observed it if it was not common practice.

Even Amali, our landlady, is under my suspicion now. Mary does not like me to talk about it, because Amali has been so nice to us, but recent events have got me wondering about her. Amali told us that her maid Dilipa had decided that she wanted to quit and look for work elsewhere, even though that meant her giving up a job she had had since 1993 and moving out of her rent free home at the back of Amali's garden. It all sounded so implausible. This morning I received a handwritten note from Dilipa, thanking me and Mary for 'treating her like a human being' and that she now lives just around the corner if we to hear of anyone looking for home help. She also went on to say that Madam Amali had worked her 17 hours a day, making her clean and cook and wait after them, with no time off, 'not even for an hour on a Sunday'. When Dilipa complained once about it, Amali allegedly screamed at her 'who are you to be making suggestions to me!' and sacked her on the spot. There are two sides to every story, but, if I need to make a judgement, I am inclined to go with Dilipa after having seen how the rich treat those who they consider beneath them. And more importantly, why would Dilipa give up her job without having anything else lined up? I would like to investigate further but I have been warned by Mary never to mention the letter to Amali. Of course she is right, because Amali would fume if she ever saw what Dilipa had written to us.

I have even been subjected to occasional racism from rich Sri Lankans. I have only had two disagreements with locals since I have been here, once over a rental car when the business owner insisted on charging me extra for the time he went on holiday and so I could not return the vehicle when I wanted to, and another time at a swimming pool when I forgot to shower before jumping in and a self appointed king of the pool decided to caution me on my poor hygiene. Neither argument was what you could call feisty, but on each occasion I was reminded pretty early in proceedings that I was a foreigner, not a Sri Lankan, and I was only a guest in this country and that I should not forget it. It seemed to me that they both resorted to unnecessary racist language quite readily. I wonder to what extent this kind of thinking is ingrained? I know of other examples: friends of ours lived here for over four years and their neighbours point blank refused to acknowledge their existence, despite repeated attempts to be neighbourly. Finally, one day, one of the neighbours told my friends that they did not like having foreigners living anywhere near them. On another occasion at a pool at a hotel in Colombo, I heard a Sri Lankan woman yelling at some Western kids to get their white skin out of the Sri Lankan water. It does seem that Sri Lankans resort to this kind of language pretty quickly. Politicians engage in racist language all the time, remember Fonseca's 'Sri Lanka is for the Singhalese' comment, and of course, the whole war with the Tamils was framed along a racist and religious divide.

13

It is Poya day today, which means that the whole country has a day off, schools are shut and businesses are closed. I only know this because I headed to the supermarket for supplies and was confronted with a big smiley face on a sign that informed me I could not have any alcohol today. A Poya is a Buddhist holiday and it occurs every full moon. Each one has its own name: like Poson Poya, or Duruthu Poya or Unduvap Poya, and it is meant to be a day when Buddhists go to their temple, get all ritualistic, bang drums and light incense. Today is Navam Poya Day so happy Navam Poya to me. Seeing as it is such an important Buddhist day there is a complete ban on all meat and alcohol across the entire island. I think Sri Lanka is the only country in the world that does this. Sam loves it because he gets a day off school. I hate it because I always forget to stock up and end up being an unwilling tee-total vegetarian for the day. I really need pay more attention to the moon cycles.

Hot on the heels of the Presidential election, Sri Lanka is preparing for parliamentary elections. Huge political posters have been springing up all over the country. I read somewhere that political posters are only allowed at the office of the candidate and all other posters are technically illegal. Regardless, the whole country is awash with posters of smiling politicians, some of which are 50 feet high, and those from the same party as the President also feature a picture of the Rajapaksa in the left hand corner so it is clear whose party you need to vote for.

Meanwhile, a Sri Lankan court has ordered that six army officers suspected of plotting to overthrow the government should remain in custody. The six are suspected of being sympathetic to General Fonseca. At least 53 supporters of General Fonseca, many of them serving or retired military officials, were arrested by police after the presidential election. At least 30 of them are still behind bars. Interestingly, the government has accused one of the suspects of being involved in the assassination of Lasantha Wickramathunga, the newspaper editor who predicted his own murder in an editorial last year. You have got to hand it to the Sri Lankan government. They really know how to stitch someone up.

General Fonseca is to face court martial proceedings for engaging in politics while in uniform and for breaking army procurement rules. On the face of it, these charges do not appear to be too serious, but the government is still pursuing the far more significant charge that the General was also plotting a coup and the assassination of President Rajapaksa. The General has denied it all and wants to stand in the parliamentary election. He has objected to the judging panel because it included two men that he had disciplined when he ran the army and the third member was a close relative of the current army commander who initiated the court martial. It seems like a legitimate complaint to me but the objection was overruled, (by the presiding panel naturally).

14

My motorbike has been making some strange backfiring noises, which may be because some old man at the petrol station decided to add 2T oil to my petrol when I was not looking. This 2T oil is added to tuc-tucs and smaller engine mopeds, but not TVS Victors like mine, so he must have been daydreaming or or something. In any case, after I yelled and waved at him to stop and he realized his mistake, his answer was to tip my bike over and pour the offending petrol/oil mix all over the petrol station forecourt before topping up my tank up with petrol again. I was amazed that the bike started but the old petrol attendant looked at me like I was a fool to doubt his ways. I am sure he pours petrol and oil mixes all over the petrol station forecourt all the time.

In any case, since the bike had started backfiring loudly, and since the noise is not too different to that of a firing rifle, which is not something I am keen to recreate with so many soldiers around, I thought I would head to the TVS service centre for a check-up. This immediately marks me out as a foreigner as locals do not go to mechanics for 'check-ups'. The general motto seems to be if it is moving, then it is fine. There is no concept of a MOT here. I once saw a man on Galle Road driving a tuc-

tuc with no roof, no seat, (he was sitting on a upturned bucket), and no fuel tank, (he had a litre of petrol in a coca cola bottle on the back seat with a thin plastic pipe leading from the bottle to his engine). He was not taking it easy either. He flew past me tootling his horn and swerving in and out of the moving traffic, swishing the petrol in his coke bottle about and making his upside down bucket slide from side to side.

Driving to the TVS service centre is always an exciting adventure as it involves driving along Dr. Danister de Silva Mawatha, otherwise known as Baseline Road for those of us who struggle with polysyllabic names for streets. Baseline Road is one of the few roads in Sri Lanka where cars can pick up some speed, and even has triple lanes for a stretch of four or five miles. This makes for a thrilling ride with everyone keen to see how much they can squeeze out of the engine.

To add to the excitement today, there were two large elephants trundling along in the inside lane, while cars, trucks, bikes and tuc-tucs all honked furiously for them to get out of the way. The elephants must have seen it all before because they looked completely unfazed by the manic driving all around them and only listened to the words of their mahout as they nudged them onwards down the busy road. The elephants did not just wander into Colombo from the countryside. They were here for the Perahera, a big Sri Lankan festival full of dancers, fire eaters, drums, noise and flag waving, and of course elephants.

The Esala Perahera in Kandy is the biggest and most famous in the country but the Duruthu Perahera in Colombo is also very popular. It involves at least fifty elephants who get all cleaned and dressed up in bright costumes to participate in a religious parade that celebrates the Buddha's visit to Sri Lanka. The elephant that gets to carry the holy Buddha relic is revered almost as much as the relic itself. Hoards of devotees run along in front laying down cloth so that the elephant does not need to soil his big flat feet on the road. In our first year here, we were warned not to attend the festival as it was considered a prime target for the Tamil Tigers. We went in our second year though, where we were treated to the sight of the holy elephant taking the largest dump imaginable in the middle of the road. Scores of old women threw off their sandals, ran out into the street and jumped up and down barefoot in the huge mound of holy elephant shit. Apparently it is a great honour to cover yourself in steaming elephant turd if it has come from a sacred elephant arsehole.

The elephants on Baseline Road had shed their costumes and were presumably on the way home after finishing up at the Perahera. It is nice to see elephants randomly like this, even though they did cause an almighty distraction on the road. Working elephants are a fairly common sight in the countryside, but they are much rarer in the city. As I slowed to take a look, I was almost flattened by a truck bearing down on me with 'PTC: Priyankara Transport Company: offices in London, New York and Kurunegala' painted amateurishly on the side: and 'Danger! Highly Dangerous Truck' written in marker pen next to a crude drawing of a pirate skull and crossbones on the back. The truck screeched, skidded and honked loudly as a young kid in the passenger seat stuck his head out of the window and gave a huge, grinning 'Woo Hooo!' before the truck sped off again in front of me.

I did hear a rare uplifting story when I was at the TVS service centre. All the TVS mechanics were crowded around an old motorbike, tuning and polishing and oiling the machine with zealous care and attention. The service centre owner had brought the bike in and and one of the mechanics told me the story surrounding it. It was a British 1953 BSA Bantam motorbike and it had recently been rescued from being buried deep underground in Jaffna for the last 30 years. Apparently, a friend of the service centre manager lived in Jaffna and when the Tamil Tigers took over that part of the country in the eighties and they commandeered all the vehicles for the war effort, the BSA Bantam had been dismantled, wrapped in oily rags and buried deep in the jungle to avoid being requisitioned. When the Tiger leadership finally left Jaffna the bike had been dug up and put back together again. The service centre manager had been helping him get a replacement seat from a specialist dealer in the UK. The original Bantam leather seat had rotted away, but everything else was in perfect working order. You have to hand it to British craftsmanship - the bike still works after being buried in the tropics for a quarter of a century. I bet you could not say the same about my TVS Victor.

15

My neighbour has just returned from a trip to India and he was telling me this morning about the security checks at Colombo airport. He made it sound more like entering a high security prison than an airport. First, everyone is stopped at a check point around half a mile outside the perimeter of the airport where the army check everyone's passports. After that, guards at the entrance to the terminal building check passports a second time along with your tickets. After that, all of your bags are scanned before you are allowed to proceed to check-in, where they are scanned again. Next, your boarding card is checked by the army once more before you can line up to go through departure immigration, followed by a last security check at the departure gate where you need to empty your pockets, remove your shoes and take off your belt while showing airport staff your passport and boarding card for a final time.

Is this all because of 9/11? It must be, because I can remember when airports were not so rigorously guarded. I once turned up at Lagos airport to find that there were no immigration officers at all and there was completely unguarded access into the country. My fellow passengers tried to call for someone's attention, but we were ignored for nearly an hour and eventually we all gave up and wandered into Nigeria without an immigration check or a stamp in our passport. It caused me some problems when I tried to leave, as there was no official stamp that said I had arrived in the first place. However, that turned out to be the least of my worries, as hanging over the Ghana Airways check-in counter for my flight back to Abidjan was an A4 piece of paper with 'No Flying Today' scribbled on it. After a lot of asking around, I concluded that my options were to stay in Lagos for another week and hope that Ghana Airways would be flying next time, or to chance my luck with Air Afrique, a West African airline that was on the Foreign Office list of airlines not to use even in the direst of circumstances. Given that the Nigerians were increasingly curious to know how I had got into the country illegally, I decided that Air Afrique was worth the risk and spent the entire flight buckled in with white knuckles until we landed safely in Abidjan.

Over the years I travelled quite a few of these unconventional routes on less well known airlines and it always occurred to me that these were the types of flights that went down all the time with no-one back home batting an eyelid. You can imagine the ten second excerpt on the BBC: 'Today an Air Afrique flight en route to Abidjan from the Nigerian capital Lagos crashed just after take-off. Authorities say that 226 people have died and there are reports that there was one British national on board'.

On another flight in Africa, this time from Nairobi to Kinshasa, I travelled with USD 50,000 in a small diplomatic bag with me in the cabin because the British embassy in the Congo had run out of foreign currency and needed it to keep paying their bills. The Congo government had put all sorts of restrictions on transfers of foreign currency even though nobody in Kinshasa wanted to deal with anything other than US dollars. The situation had got so bad that the embassy had virtually run out of cash. They called London, who called us in Nairobi, with orders to stick a bundle of notes in a diplomatic bag and have someone fly to

Kinshasa, meet someone from the embassy staff, hand over the cash and then return to Nairobi on the same flight.

When I stepped off the plane in the Congo, I walked over the tarmac through a small door into the airport, straight through the unguarded immigration and customs into a busy terminal building, out into a busy street beyond to meet my colleague and hand over the bag with the fifty grand. I returned to the plane using the same route, past soldiers and Kenya Airways officials, straight past immigration and check-in and got back onto the plane without being asked for my passport or ticket once. 9/11 may have changed the security procedures at many airports all over the world, but my guess is that at Lagos and Kinshasa airports things have not changed all that much.

I actually volunteered to take the trip because I liked the idea of flying over the middle of Africa from east to west and back again in one day. My Nairobi-Kinshasa-Nairobi direct service actually took in an unexpected and unannounced pick-up stop in Douala, Cameroon, which came as a bit of a shock because no one at Kenya Airways had mentioned that we were calling in at Cameroon on the way and I thought we were landing at Kinshasa (hundreds of miles from the coast) until I looked out the window and saw us banking over the Atlantic Ocean.

But, on the journey home we followed the path of the milk chocolate coloured Congo river as it wound its way slowly through the huge jungles of the Congo basin. Jungle stretched out in every direction as far as the eye could see. The only interruption to the endless view of trees came from an occasional plume of smoke, which may have been from villages or could have been from explosions, because at the very moment I was crossing the Congo by air, Laurent Kabila was edging his rebel forces across the jungle below towards Kinshasa where a few months later he would overthrow the dictatorship of President Mobutu and become President of the Congo himself.

This was in 1996 and still, fourteen years later, the conflict in the Eastern Congo continues. The region is largely ignored by the International Community despite some estimates putting the number of those killed at 5.4 million, making it the world's deadliest conflict since the Second World War. The conflict started when tensions between Hutus and Tutsis in neighbouring Rwanda spilled over into the Congo. (The commonly quoted figure of causalities in the Rwandan Civil War is usually quoted at around 800,000. The numbers are quite staggering). Fleeing Rwandan Hutu militia forces, the Interahamwe, joined forces with local Congolese armed forces to launch attacks against Congolese Tutsis. In turn, Tutsi led governments in Uganda and Rwanda launched armies of their own under the cover of a Tutsi militia group. They were soon joined by various Congolese politicians who were keen to overthrow Congo's longstanding dictator Mobutu and get their hands on some of Congo's huge mineral resources of diamonds, copper and zinc. One of these Congolese politicians was Laurent Kabila and he led the Tutsi coalition of forces to victory in Kinshasa before naming himself President. However, fearful of a mutiny against him from his assortment of armed forces, Kabila quickly asked all foreign forces to leave the country, which annoyed the Rwandans and Ugandans, who were keen to exert some of their influence over the big, mineral rich neighbour. Competing militias were launched, one by the Rwandans and another by the Ugandans and they both attacked the Congolese army. Other African countries were drawn into the conflict on the side of the Congolese government.

Laurent Kabila was assassinated in 2001 to be succeeded by his son, Joseph, and he remains President to this day. But the problems in the Eastern Congo persist as militias, rebellions and counter insurgencies continue to ravage the area with ethnic cleansing and conflict to control mineral resources. Stories of armed forces shooting innocent civilians or committing sexual violence are tragically all too common. In a recent documentary called 'The Greatest Silence', about rape in the Congo, it is alleged that 200,000 women have been raped in the last decade. In a more specific example of the daily atrocities that occur there, the UN recently documented a four-day attack on the eastern town of Luvungi and nearby villages, where three groups of armed militia raped 235 women, 52 girls, 13 men and three boys, many of them multiple times. The militias looted more than 900 houses and abducted 116 people. Sadly, the world pays very little attention to these outrages.

As a footnote to the way air travel has changed, consider this story. A few years ago I sat next to a French woman on a flight from Abidjan to Paris who asked me to look after her handbag while she went to the bathroom at the back of the plane. I did think that was a little strange. Why would a complete stranger ask me to look after her handbag? She left the small, square, shiny, black leather designer bag on her seat and as soon as she had gone, a little chihuahua dog popped out his head and quickly looked around. Before I could react, he jumped out and crawled into a small crevice under her seat. It was a night flight and most of the cabin was in darkness with sleeping passengers, but in the gloom at 30,000 feet I was stretching under a French woman's seat fumbling around for a little dog with a big red furry collar. Every time I grabbed the collar to try and pull him out, the little chihuahua snapped and yipped making me pull back my hand. Eventually I grabbed one of his back legs and pulled him out backwards, with him desperately clawing the floor to try and get back under the seat. I stuffed him roughly back into the bag and buttoned it shut just moments before the French woman returned. Of course I asked her about the dog and whether it is was okay to carry a dog in a handbag on the plane, but she looked at me incredulously and said, 'Non, I have no dog in the bag' and then pulled down her eye mask and went to sleep clutching the bag on her lap.

16

There is a lot of discussion in Colombo about whether the General should be tried in a military court or whether he should be tried in a civilian court because he has now left the military. I think the suggestion is that the General would get a fairer hearing in a civilian court, which is why his supporters are annoyed at the government's decision to court martial him in a military court. I am sure that the government would prefer to keep him locked away on a military base rather than have him tried in a public courtroom.

I saw a lot of courtrooms and prison cells in one of my former jobs with the Foreign Office. For three years I was the vice consul in Barbados. I know, it sounds fantastic: Barbados, white sands, azure seas, rum shacks and reggae. Yet we could not wait to leave. For a holiday, two or three weeks, then certainly it is a nice place to visit, but after three years we had developed a serious case of island fever. Many long term expats there will tell you the same thing: once the excitement of the beach wears off, you realize that you are marooned on an island you can drive around in a morning with little to do but try to cope with the incredibly insular, rude and surly attitude of the people on the island, the Bajans. Barbados Tourist websites will tell you the opposite, that the locals will give you a warm and friendly welcome with a sincere smile. But I found Bajans to be, by and large, an incredibly unfriendly bunch. Alongside the hotels of the west coast or the pubs and restaurants of the south, the people rely on tourism and are superficially pleasant. Go inland and away from the tourism industry and attitudes to outsiders are quite different. There is no warm and friendly welcome here. If you need to stop for any kind of supplies forget any concept of customer service. There will be no greeting, no eye contact during conversations and plenty of disparaging remarks about people not from their little rock. The antipathy also includes people from neighbouring islands, so people from Trinidad or Guyana are treated as much of an alien as someone from England. The hostility of the inter-island rivalry within the West Indies came as a big shock to me. They all seem to hate each other. You could not help but feel that the Bajans would be happier if they could expel everyone not born on Barbados from their island. They only put up with the holiday makers because their entire economy depends on it. The local staff at the High Commission were just as bad. I was forever answering calls from irate Brits who had been on the receiving end of typical Bajan unfriendliness, such as tutting loudly down the line at someone making an enquiry, or telling callers to call back another time as they had 'jus' too much doing'.

As vice consul, I had to assist British holiday makers when they got themselves into trouble. Most of it was straightforward, like an overnight arrest for smoking a joint on the beach, followed by a brief court appearance and your photo and name published on the front page of the local newspaper, 'The Nation'. Most of the younger tourists thought it was fantastic to get your name in the paper and would ensure they got a copy of it to take home and show their friends. Headlines next to a photograph of the tourist leaving the courtroom would inevitably say things like, 'John Smith, a British visitor to the

Island, leaving court yesterday after being fined GBP100 for possession of marijuana'.

However, other Brits got themselves into much bigger trouble by trying to smuggle cocaine back to the UK in large quantities. At one point there were 35 British tourists in Glendairy Prison in Bridgetown, and I was their only contact with the outside world. At least half of them were women. Many had been approached in the UK and promised a free holiday if they brought back some cocaine. Others did it because they were addicts and needed the cash. One such addict, Benny, was arrested at the airport and taken to Oistens police station, which was the nearest station to the airport with proper holding cells. When I visited him, he barely registered my presence as he was coming down from some concoction of drugs. I could not give legal advice or anything like that, but it was my job to make sure he knew what had happened, what was likely to happen, to give him a list of local lawyers and ask whether he needed me to contact any friends or family or someone else on his behalf, that sort of thing. All Benny would say was that he was not guilty. It was a stitch up and he had no cocaine on him at all. A Bajan police officer overhead all this so he walked over with Benny's suitcase and opened it on the table in front of us before pulling out at least seven or eight kilo bags of cocaine. There was white powder all over table and Benny's eyes lit up, before he composed himself a little and muttered that 'none of that is mine'. Benny went down for five years, but he later told me that he had previously done some prison time in Turkey, so for him, Barbados was a breeze.

Others were less hardened and really did not understand the arrest process at all, which made my job much harder. I would have to accompany them to the courtroom and then explain to them that they were going to prison for x amount of years. It came as quite a surprise to quite a few Brits, who just assumed that foreign law did not apply to them, or I would be able to somehow get them off.

In the Bridgetown law courts, the judge opened proceedings at 10am, but there was no schedule as such, or certainly there was nothing published, so you just needed to wait your turn and listen to all the cases beforehand. The public areas were always packed with family members or more usually with old women who came in to hear some gossip. Barbados was a small society where everyone knew everyone else. Court appearances were apparently great for good, cheap entertainment and a way of spreading scandals.

Usually I struggled to stay awake through the stories: Denzil Brathwaite has threatened a police officer while under the influence of rum, or Anne-Marie Dawkins had beaten her husband with a cricket bat again. Occasionally though, a case came before the judge that livened up the morning: for example, one day while I was waiting to hear the charges against another Brit who had attempted to smuggle cocaine, I heard the police prosecutor begin outlining a case against a local man who had been arrested at Brown's Beach for masturbating in public in the midday sun. A row of old women behind me erupted into jeering laughter, with a few cries of 'My Lord!' and 'Sweet Jesus!' thrown in for good measure. The judge made no attempt to calm the court; instead he appeared rather to be enjoying the fun. He kept making mock looks of astonishment to the court, and made a big dramatic show of burying his head in his hands. He eventually asked the accused what he had to say for himself, and the man looked down sheepishly and said in an embarrassed and quiet voice that he thought he was alone and he would not have done anything like that if he had known people were around and could see him. The police prosecutor then stood up again and said that according to the police report, the man had been warned three times to stop masturbating before he had eventually been arrested. The courtroom erupted once more, with the old ladies behind me slapping the wooden benches with glee and even courtroom officials and guards bent over double with laughter. Even the judge was laughing uproariously. The press photographer flash was repeatedly lighting up the courtroom as he made sure he got his front-page picture for the next day's paper. The judge finally decided that the public humiliation was punishment enough because the accused was let off with a warning not to go back to Brown's Beach and a reminder to resist the temptation to touch himself in public from now on.

In general, sentences were much more lenient in Barbados than they would have been for the same offence in the UK. For example, being caught with five kilos of cocaine in the UK could lead to a sentence of 14 or 15 years, but in Barbados it normally got you five years, reduced to four with good behaviour. Sometimes, if you played the system the right way, you could get away with much less than that.

This happened to a young kid who was half Nigerian and half British, (but since the Nigerians did not have any kind of representation in Barbados, it was me who got the call from the police). They called to say that they had arrested someone, traveling with a Nigerian passport, but claiming to be British, and that he would be taken to the Queen Elizabeth hospital, and not Oistens police station, because he had swallowed 75 packets of cocaine. My immediate reaction was, of course, to try and promote his Nigerian-ness, so that I could avoid another prisoner to take care of. The police however, found his British passport in his luggage and so I was obliged to add him to my list of inmates. This sounds a bit callous, but it is how vice consuls think.

Finding patients in Barbados hospitals was always a chore. There were no admission records and you had to walk from ward to ward asking the nurses if there were any British people in. On any given day, there are dozens of cruise ships in the port, full of elderly British holiday makers. It was a fairly regular event for some of them to be hospitalized at some point, and mostly the cruise ships or travel agent would take care of everything, so there was no need for me get involved. However, the nurses did not know the difference and they used to send me to anyone they thought might be from Britain. It used to take me ages wandering from aged cruise ship Brit to aged cruise ship Brit before I found the patient I was looking for. Sometimes it was incredibly difficult to get away from the old dears once they knew that someone from the High Commission was there to see them and I had to fob them off with fake tales of incredibly important imminent James Bond type missions to take care of.

On this occasion, it was much easier than usual, because all the nurses knew where I could find the boy who had swallowed 75 condoms filled with cocaine. 'He in there' said one nurse, pointing in the direction of a bed with a curtain pulled round for privacy. The rest of the ward was full, and all the patients and their visitors were up and alert and trying to peek a look inside the curtain every time someone moved and the curtain twitched a little. I walked over and pulled back the curtain to find a young man on the bed, stark naked on all fours, surrounded by doctors, nurses and police, including one with a camera. One of the nurses held a small metal tray with numerous packets of cocaine on it, all smeared in excrement and blood, and every time the young man squeezed out another one of the packets from his arse, the police photographer took a series of photographs to record the passage. There were around 40 packets in a box on the side of the bed, so he was about half-way through his photo session when I turned up.

It is pretty hard to discuss court procedures, lawyers, family contact numbers etc, when your client is shitting out small packets of cocaine, but that is what we did for the next hour or so. The poor guy was only 20 and he gave me the number of his older brother, who he thought could help him out of this mess. When I got back to the office I called the older brother and explained what had happened. I usually dreaded these calls. Giving bad news over the phone from thousands of miles away is never easy. Reactions ranged from loud sobs to angry silence, (although in the case of Terry the cocaine smuggler, I seem to remember that his partner snorted and said that she 'wasn't surprised the useless bastard had done it again'). On this occasion though, the older brother calmly took in all the details I gave him, thanked me and then said he would be in touch. Two days later he was in my office in Bridgetown, asking who the judge was going to be who would hear the case and asking me for a list of local lawyers. After that, he said he would not need any more help from me and that he planned to stay until this was all sorted out, having put himself up in a small guesthouse in Bridgetown. I was pleasantly surprised at all this self-sufficiency from the older brother because most of the time other family members that came out to Barbados needed a lot of assistance in finding accommodation and setting up prison meetings. I was happy to let him get on with it.

I went along to the first court hearing and sat next to the older brother and his lawyer and was quite surprised when the lawyer stood up and entered a plea of not guilty. Even the judge looked surprised. I mean, I had seen him shitting out the cocaine myself. So had a dozen doctors, nurses, police officers, fellow patients and most of their visitors. There were even a series of 75 photographs to submit as evidence. How could he plead not guilty?

Clearly though, something was being agreed behind the scenes. There were three more hearings and at each one the case was adjourned and the accused pleaded not guilty. Then suddenly, at a fourth hearing, the lawyer abruptly changed tact and pleaded guilty. The judge called me to his table and asked me, (me!) if I thought that a fine of USD10,000 would be acceptable. I told him that it had nothing to do with me, but yes, that sounded like a good deal for the accused. And that is how the deal was struck. Bizarrely, when handing down the sentence, the judge made some remarks about Barbados having a responsibility to its 'African brothers' to be lenient in these types of cases. In fact, the court was even more lenient than it intended because the court clerk misheard the judge and entered the sentence as a fine of Bajan dollars 10,000 and not USD 10,000, which meant that they had to pay a fraction of the agreed amount. The older brother pulled out his wallet, they paid the fine in cash and disappeared on the next flight out of Barbados.

17

If there is one thing that I will never get used to in Sri Lanka it is the complete lack of regard for personal space. Cars literally brush past you when they overtake on the road; people on the street often bang into you as they walk past; on an escalator, the person behind you will try and share the same step if they can; if you are sitting on a wall, or a bench, someone else will come and sit so close that your thighs rub together. Cars make no allowance as they drive past pedestrians, so they regularly hit arms or hands as they pass by. If we are sitting in a completely empty restaurant, a Sri Lankan waiter will sit any new arrivals as close to us as possible. If I am waiting on my bike at traffic lights, or coloured lights as they are often referred to here, another biker will manoeuvre so close that our knees will be touching. Several times, I have had to move my foot quickly to stop it from being run over.

A visit to the post office here always reminds me of how I miss orderly queues and respect for personal space. The Sri Lanka post office in Borella is hidden behind two or three noisy bus stops in a dark and windowless, musty building. Getting past the buses and the multitude of passengers struggling to embark and disembark is always a challenge, but usually I can ride my bike up on to the pavement and park it right outside the door, scattering a few pedestrians in the process.

It is incredibly dark inside and there are no signs or information about prices or which counter to go to. The only thing that is recognisable is a big framed photograph of His Excellency the President, looking all regal and happy. You really have to guess what you need to do until you learn the system. It is only through time-consuming trial and error that I know that the counter I need to get my parcel weighed is the third from the left, and the one where I buy the stamps is the second from the right. Sending parcels is cheap, but for some reason the smallest denomination of stamp is a fraction of the postage price so you still need to stick at least thirty stamps on the outside of any parcel. I have taken to writing the address really small to allow room for all the licking and sticking. Incidentally, the currency in Sri Lanka smells incredibly bad. It is old, horribly grubby and smells like it has been shoved for safe keeping down endless pairs of underpants and sarongs, which of course, it undoubtedly has. There is also a severe shortage of it. Try and pay with any note higher than 100 Rupees, (around 1 US dollar) and the shopkeeper will always ask, and I mean ALWAYS ask, if you have anything smaller. Tuc-tuc drivers are even worse. They never have change for any amount. If you get a ride home you better make sure you have exactly the right fare. Credit cards, which are so common in the Western world, are rarely used here. Hardly any shops will accept payment with any kind of card and the very few that do charge you 5 per cent extra for the privilege. It is a cash only society with a shortage of notes.

I needed to visit the post office today because I wanted to send a couple of DVDs to my parents. The person behind me in the queue for the counter got so close to me that I could actually feel his groin pushing against my backside. No amount of turning and glaring could get him to stop, and in any case, I was preoccupied with keeping my place because other people were cutting in front and pushing in from the sides. Little old women are always the worst at this. At first I used to show respect for gender and age, but being on the receiving end of one or two sharp jabs from the elderly soon evened the playing field as far as I was concerned. It is everyone for themselves in a Sri Lankan queue.

You need to jostle to maintain your position even when you get to the front of the counter because when you are in discussion with the clerk about weight, destination and price, there is usually an almighty struggle going on just behind you to secure the next position. It is shameful to admit, but on one particularly hot and humid day, after a really long struggle to get to the counter, I lost it completely after I was repeatedly barged into from behind while I was trying to get the right number of Rupees out of my pocket to post a letter to England. Hot, sweaty and frustrated, I turned round sharply and snarled menacingly for everyone to 'Back the fuck off!'. This created such a stir that everyone moved back at least three feet away from me. Sure, they all thought I was a crazy foreign psycho, but at the time I thought it was a small price to pay.

Today there was an additional problem because I had written 'contents: 2 DVDs' on the outside of the parcel. An innocent sort of comment on a parcel you would think, but the Borella post office took immediate exception to it. The clerk looked at me, then back at the parcel, then back at me and then bashed the counter with his hand a few times before he informed me that it was not allowed to send any DVDs outside of Sri Lanka. And that was that. No more discussion. Next customer please. The crush behind me began in earnest and I was quickly jostled to one side and out of the way.

I wanted to find out what the problem was with sending DVDs so I starting looking around for someone in charge. All the counters were packed with pushing people, so I wandered to the far wall, looked over a small divider and saw a dozens of people sitting at tables writing things longhand in large ledger books. Without invitation I wandered in and asked for the boss.

Most people looked up uninterested, but one man looked up from behind a large pile of papers and indicated that I should take a seat at his table. He was quite an officious looking man with slightly overly coiffed grey hair and when he stood up I could see that he was only a little man and that his trousers were perched and belted just a little bit too high up. He reminded me of Noel Edmonds on Deal or No Deal.

'It is an impossibility to be sending any DVDs from this office' Sri Lankan Noel informed me. 'This is from the government. It is a security situation. If you want to send a DVD you must go to the post office in Pettah district and get special permission from there. You must then return here with your permission and we will send your parcel.'

I sighed with frustration. How on earth could sending a couple of DVDs be a 'security situation'? Also, I did not want to go to Pettah. It is an awful place to get to, jammed full of traffic, pollution, noise and beggars with nowhere to park. I tried to reason with Sri Lankan Noel, but each time I opened my mouth, he looked to the side and engaged in conversation with someone else, or picked up the phone to make a call, or called a cleaner over to bring him a glass of water. He was incredibly rude and dismissive and intent on ignoring me. Yet, I had nothing else to do so I sat resolutely by his desk, patiently interrupting him about the possibility of sending the DVDs. Eventually I persuaded him that if he opened the package and personally checked the DVDs then he could confirm that there was nothing sinister about them. It was only the latest series of '24' which I had bought a pirate copy of for 5 dollars. Eventually, Noel allowed me to unpick all the sellotape I had used to reinforce the parcel and after he examined the DVDs he decided that sending '24' to my parents would not be a security risk to Sri Lanka, as long as I gave him my passport details. ID is such a big issue in Sri Lanka that I never went anywhere without a photocopy of my passport, so I was able to fish out my passport details with a flourish. Noel began to slowly and deliberately copy down my name, place of birth and passport number in a huge ledger book and while he did so I stealthily pinched some sellotape from his desk and began to wrap up my parcel again.

When he had finished with his ledger book he waved his hand to indicate I could go back to the counter and send my parcel. Feeling quite proud that I had accomplished this seemingly hopeless task, I headed back to the queues and rejoined the shoving crowd with my parcel. When I got to the clerk I got the inevitable rejection, but this time I was ready, I had permission to send.

I smiled at the clerk and said, 'It's okay. The man over, the man who looks like Noel Edmonds, he wrote down my name in a book and he says I can send this parcel'.

But the clerk continued to shake his head and he repeated 'It is not allowed to send DVDs outside of Sri Lanka'

'No, it is' I implored, pointing in the direction of Sri Lankan Noel.

'It is not' said the clerk.

'Ask him over there!' I said, pointing to where the boss had been sitting, but Sri Lankan Noel had now left, and his desk was empty. The clerk looked over my shoulder for the next customer and I was quickly bundled out of the way again. Depressed, I wandered into the office and left the parcel and a note with 'Could you send this please?' on Sri Lankan Noel's desk. Who knows if it will ever reach its destination.

18

While a visit to the post office is an experience that always requires a fight to the counter and an acceptance that others will push and jab you out the way, it is still nothing compared to getting on a Sri Lankan train. The first time we got on a train was at Maradana station, where someone had told us it was easier, because it was one stop before Fort station, the busiest station in Sri Lanka where it is difficult to get on or off. Congratulating ourselves on our astuteness, we checked the timetables and made our way to Maradana to buy tickets and get on our train to Galle.

Galle is on the south west tip of Sri Lanka and reached the height of its importance in the eighteenth century when the Dutch used it as a trading port and built a large fort to defend it. The fort is still there, a world heritage site, and remains one of the largest and best preserved European fortresses in Asia. Galle is a still a major town by Sri Lankan standards and if you want to go to the south and spend time at one of the beaches, you generally need to take a bus or a train that passes through Galle.

We set off for Maradana station in the expectation that we had cleverly calculated that we could jump on board and bag three seats before the crush of commuters took over the train. However, Maradana was a heaving mass of humanity with no information signs and the only announcements were from a tinny tannoy in Sinhala. We had to ask dozens of people which one was the train for Galle, and as each train pulled in, people around us shook their heads, or told us to wait for the next one. As each train stopped, we watched people fight to get off and fight to get on at the same time. There was no concept of letting passengers disembark first, and each stop looked increasingly like a bar brawl as people began to swing arms and push in an attempt to get on or off the train. It looked near impossible to get on the train, never mind stay together as a group and hang on to Mary and Sam at the same time. When the Galle train finally arrived all our new friends on the platform pointed and nodded, shouting 'Galle, Galle'. Yet clearly, the Galle train was already full; in fact it was overflowing full. I was all for abandoning the train and looking for a bus but Mary had other plans and grabbed Sam's hand and barged headlong into the scrum. I was left stuck on the platform with our bag (one bag, luckily we travel light) as people swarmed around and in front of me and pushed on board. I saw the top of Mary's head amongst the people that had pushed on board and realised that I needed to catch up quickly, just as the train began to slowly pull away. In a panic, I hurled the bag over the heads of the passengers crushed into the doorway and tried to barge onboard.

 I stood on the small step on the outside of the train and held onto the two handrails that were positioned on either side of the open door but I could not squeeze in any further. I had one small Sri Lankan man under one armpit, sharing my step and one handrail, and another under the other armpit, sharing the step and the other handrail as the train pulled away from the station. Everyone was so incredibly crushed on the train but apparently this was normal because people were smiling at me and nodding, trying to strike up conversations, asking the usual questions:

'You are from?' 'You like Sri Lanka?'

I could make out Mary and Sam grinning at me through the sea of Sri Lankan heads, so I knew they were safe on board, and after my initial fear about hanging onto the outside of a moving train, I began to relax and start enjoying the moment. This was a view of Colombo that I did not normally see. Almost immediately we went through a long dark tunnel where it looked like some people had set up home and we trundled past them as they sat around fires, quite oblivious to the thundering train passing by just a few feet away.

One through the tunnel and into the sunshine again, a quick glance up and down the outside of the train showed me that I was not alone hanging on the outside. Each entrance was as equally packed as ours, and at least three or four people were hanging onto each handrail. It was so ridiculously dangerous, but here were people doing this as a commute, and they were happy about it, smiling (but not waving, both hands were needed to hold on to the side) at me as I looked their way. Gradually the tracks multiplied as various routes descended into Fort station. Just as I started to relax a little, I was startled by a loud and prolonged blast of horn that came from just behind me. Another train, moving faster than us, was on neighbouring tracks and was similarly loaded with passengers. I realised with panic that the second train was intent on overtaking, forcing those of us hanging on the side to breathe in and push up together so that we avoided the passengers hanging off the side of the passing train, who were all breathing and pushing in too. We passed within inches of one another, and the passing passengers all smiled as they went by, until we were all engulfed in black smoke as the passing train guffed out loud.

Most people wanted to get off at Fort, which made it particularly difficult for me to push against the flow, but I managed to squeeze through, picking up our bag along the way from some kind commuter who was happy to hold on to it for me as I hung on the side. As we left Colombo and the passengers thinned out, people started walking up and down the carriages, looking for seats, or singing songs or begging for money, or selling coconuts, mangoes or pineapples or a variety of warm sugary drinks in boxes. We scrambled with everyone else to find some seats and we finally settled down on our wooden bench by an open window. The beggars and singers that previously had wandered slowly down each carriage soon began to congregate around us, pestering us for money. Even the blind man seemed to know that a Western family was on the train and he managed to find us.

Each carriage had a mixture of rows of wooden seat benches and individual plastic covered seats. There were only around nine rows in total per carriage, so many people travelled standing. None of the windows had any glass in them, thankfully, as it was stifling hot. There were three big fans bolted to the ceiling of the carriage but none of them looked like they had done any cooling for many a year.

The Sri Lankan railway lines had been introduced by the British in the mid nineteenth century in an effort to unify Sri Lanka and to ease the shipment of tea from the Hill Country. These days they are primarily passenger trains that move huge amounts of people around the country, in discomfort for the most part, as there has been precious little upgrading of the railways since Independence. Although we had seats, we were often bumped off them as the ride was full of alarming and sudden jolts or lists to the side as the train rattled along. It felt like the track was missing pieces in places, such was the incredibly noisy and uncomfortable manner in which it made its way south.

People stared at us constantly, presumably unused to seeing a family of three white people on the train, (and there were no other foreigners on board that we could see). Cultural differences abounded: we had brought along a baguette, and ham and cheese and olives to eat and our neighbours stared at us with incomprehension as they unfolded their wrapped banana leaves containing curry, rice and chilli. We snacked on sweets and crisps and our neighbours ate peanuts from little plastic bags and chewed on dried red chillies. We carefully put all of our rubbish in a plastic bag and stuck it inside our bag. Our neighbours cheerfully threw their plastic water bottles, peanut bags and left over curry paper straight out of the window.

When we wanted to stretch our legs, we moved to the doorway, where previously I had been hanging for dear life, but now we were able to sit or stand on the step at leisure and enjoy the view. The tracks followed the coast all the way down the western side of the island, so on one side we had a perfect view of white sand beaches, the Indian Ocean and palm trees. On the other side we passed through what looked like, and I suspect indeed was, the middle of people's back gardens and we had completely unobstructed views straight into their homes.

As we moved south and out of the Colombo sprawl we travelled through tropical jungles and mangrove swamps and saw crocodiles bathing by the side of rivers. We passed through resorts at Hikkaduwa, Panadura, and Ambalangoda and at Kalutara, a former capital of Sri Lanka but now famous for the Kalutara Vihara, a large three story Buddhist shrine, unusual because it is hollow and is decorated with a series of 74 murals each depicting a different scene from the Buddha's life. As we slowed, everyone on the train started praying towards the huge white Vihara and we could see devotees placing food and flowers in front of the images of Buddha, lighting coconut-oil lamps, tying prayers written on scraps of cloth to one of the Bo trees or pouring water into conduits which run down to water the Bo tree's roots. We saw motorists, buses and motorcyclists stop by the side of the road to drop coins into a sequence of donation boxes that lined the roadside, praying for a safe journey. And then we were off again, finally reaching Galle on time, 4 hours later having covered the 75 mile journey.

19

Kunty the maid comes to clean today so I need to think of something to do so I can get out of the house and leave her to it. I hate being in the house when Kunty is doing the cleaning. I can never get any peace, and every time I find somewhere quiet to sit down she creeps up on me like a stealthy ninja with a feather duster. I think I just find the whole idea of having someone round to do the cleaning while I am sitting around reading or watching TV just a little uncomfortable. I would rather do without a cleaner, I really would. I would rather do all the vacuuming myself. However, Mary has decided that my version of house cleaning is not up to the required standard and I am not going to argue with that. Without question, Kunty is way ahead of me in these skills. She is a little cleaning machine. So, despite my misgivings, Kunty is here to stay.

In Sri Lanka and many other places, having someone to do the house cleaning is usually regarded as the right thing to do because it provides employment. Kunty only works here one day a week, which is as much as I can put up with, but when we were in Kenya we had a permanent live-in maid called Asha. It was around the time of that catchy song by Cornershop called 'Brimful of Asha' so I used to play it for her regularly, although it did not look as though she enjoyed it much. Asha came from the magnificently named Kakamega, in western Kenya, near Lake Victoria. When I remarked that her hometown must be near the border with Uganda, Asha looked aghast and told me, completely deadpan, for Asha was not one for joviality, that it was a very, very long way from Uganda and that was good, because Ugandans eat their babies.

    I described Asha as a permanent live-in maid, but she did not actually live in our house with us. She lived on our property in a little hut at the bottom of our garden. She had worked for my predecessor so I was morally obliged to keep her. In any case, Asha was not going anywhere, so when my predecessor left it would be more accurate to say that we came to live with Asha. She lived in her hut with her husband John and his three kids, although it was always a bit of a secret because the High Commission in Nairobi insisted that all house maid huts were single occupancy only. This was because it was common for house maids to call for their extended family in the country to come and join them in the city as soon as they landed a job. Before you knew it there would be dozens of people living in a single room at the bottom of your garden, causing all sorts of commotion and upsetting sensitive diplomats. But we kept the secret, like a modern day African Anne Frank. In fact, Asha did such a good job of keeping her husband quiet that we only found out about John one year after we had moved in. One evening I saw a thin African bloke peering through the window at my television while I was watching Nairobi TV. When I asked Asha who he was she answered in her inscrutable way that he was John, her husband, who lived in my garden.

    Mary and I loved Nairobi TV and our favourite show was 'OMO pick-a-box'. OMO is a washing powder in Kenya and it was the sponsor of the show which drew contestants into Nairobi from all over the countryside, mostly the very remote countryside. The contestants would answer a question, (not too difficult, like, for example, 'what is the capital of Kenya?', I give you a clue, you are here in it today') and then they would get to choose something from a number of boxes. Without disclosing the boxes contents, the host would start offering money in exchange for what was in the box. 'What do you want, the money or the box?' he would shout, getting the audience to join in raucously. Some of the boxes contained booby prizes, but on Nairobi TV it was impossible to know what was a valued prize and what was not. For example, we watched one old lady from the hinterland get uncontrollably excited for turning down hundreds of pounds in cash for a brand new wheelbarrow and a pair of wellington boots. She was overjoyed with the wellies and pulled them on immediately.

Most Kenyans we knew used shouting as the default volume level for any conversation. At first I used to think there was constant fighting going on in offices around me at the High Commission because normal conversations sounded so loud and aggressive to the untrained ear. Kenyans were also absolutely matter-of-fact about things Westerners tend to tiptoe round for fear of causing offence. For example, there is nothing wrong about carrying a few extra pounds in Kenya. In fact, many people regarded being fat as a bit of a status symbol, presumably as it indicated you had the resources to keep yourself well fed. I first came across this when I was introducing a new staff member at the High Commission to her colleagues. They were all Kenyan women, and one of them looked at the new recruit with a flicker of recognition.

'Did you used to go to the church on Langata road?' she asked (or shouted, technically speaking) at the new woman. 'Ah, yes, I thought so. I did not recognize you at first because now you are so big and fat'.

The new woman was thrilled with the compliment. How different would that remark have been interpreted in the west?

Kenya was our first taste of real Africa and extreme poverty. We saw for the first time the kind of destitution that big African cities can generate. The Kibera slum in the middle of the city seemed to stretch on for miles, riding up and over ridges and off into the distance. It was a large sea of rusted brown corrugated metal, revolting smells and rising smoke. According to the UN based in Nairobi, who were always highly visible riding around the slum in their pristine white Toyota Landcruisers, the people who lived there made less than an average of a dollar a day. Kibera was home to over a million people when we lived there, and today it is closer to two (about the size of Philadelphia) making it the joint biggest slum in Africa along with Soweto in South Africa. There are few schools in Kibera, clean water is scarce, assault and rape are common and HIV is rampant.

Such poverty inevitably leads to high crime, and Nairobi was, and remains, a truly violent city with scant regard for life. On our first arrival driving into Nairobi from Jomo Kenyatta Airport we had to swerve past a prostrate young boy on the road, who, judging by the grotesque position he was lying in, was dead. Anticipating my question, our driver merely nodded to acknowledge that he had seen the boy and told us without any emotion that the kid had likely been run down by a car or a truck and left there. If anyone stopped to see how he was then they would be responsible for his hospital bills, so he would just stay there until a family member could come and get him.

Violent crime was everywhere. Just months before we arrived one of the staff from the High Commission had been shot in his car, and later died in the UK as a result of his injuries. While we were there, the wife of another member of staff was shot in the leg by a bullet through her car door, but she managed to keep on driving and escape her would be attacker. Carjacking, theft on the street, stealing through an open window as you drove your car through slow traffic, or armed burglary at your home were all common.

While locking the car door outside a shop, a boy no older than 7 or 8 jumped onto Mary's back and snatched a thin gold chain she was wearing. She spun round quickly and grabbed his arm, and as she did so, was joined by a Kenyan adult who had witnessed the attack. Immediately, the stranger started to hit the child hard across the face, and kept on asking Mary, 'What shall we do with him, what shall we do with him?' The stranger clearly wanted to exact some kind of public retribution, which was common in Nairobi. On my first morning at work I had looked out over the city from a window at the embassy's nineteenth floor office and seen a circle of people below setting upon someone, kicking and punching relentlessly. It was public retribution. If someone was caught engaging in petty crime, the public dished out the punishment themselves. Mary was aware of this, and so she insisted that the small boy was let go, much to the disappointment of the man who came to her assistance and wanted to teach him a lesson. This happened near our home and so over the next three years Mary and I saw that small boy fairly regularly. He would grin at us from a distance and ask us for change, but never tried any more snatches. He presumably thought that we would be less inclined to prevent his beating if he was caught a second time. In any case, Mary gave up wearing any kind of jewellery for the rest of our time in Kenya.

Most expats there referred to the city as 'Nairobbery'. At our embassy owned house in Westlands, we had 24 hour guards and twenty feet high fences with razor wire to keep the robbers out. We also had a huge bullet proof security door that we slept behind every night so that if intruders somehow made their way in, then at least we would be safe behind the bullet proof door. The protection of our outer perimeter depended entirely on the professionalism of our night guard, Timiteo, an aged and retired Kenyan army soldier who gave us a triple stamp salute every time we came home and he opened the gates. Mary suspected Timiteo of sleeping at night, which of course defeated the purpose of having a guard in the first place. One night around 10pm she shouted out of the window, 'Timiteo, are you asleep?' to which he replied, 'Not yet, Madam!' What he lacked in guarding skills, he made up for with honesty. In any case, we liked Timiteo (and his triple stamp salute) and we wanted to build a bond with him. Home attacks were common because the contracted security guards earned so little each month that gangs found it easy to bribe them to open the gates, thus rendering the fences and razor wire completely useless. It was therefore good practice to strike up a good connection with your guards in the hope that they would stay loyal. We fed Timiteo, gave him clothes, paid him bonuses and treated him well, yet there was always a risk that he would be tempted by a bribe. This happened to friends of ours from the Netherlands, who had lived in Kenya for years and had kept the same guard and fed and clothed him for their entire posting, just like us and Timiteo. Yet one night, their guard opened the gates to a gang who robbed our friends at gun point, a husband, wife and two young girls, before packing everything of value in our friend's car and driving off. The gang left the wife and children tied up at home, but took the husband, forcing him into the boot of his own car before they dropped him off in a forest outside Nairobi at night. All the while, his wife and kids feared that he had been kidnapped or killed. Luckily they all survived, but they were so traumatized by the ordeal that they left the country immediately.

Our next door neighbors also left the country prematurely and at short notice after their kids stood by their gate and witnessed a machete fight in the street over a disagreement over 50 shillings, which was the equivalent of around 50 pence. People came running out of their houses to cheer on the two protagonists as they took chunks out of each other with their axes. The machete battle ended when the brother of one of the fighters turned up in his matatu blaring the horn and scattering the throng.

Matatus are Kenyan minibuses, with the most daring drivers in Kenya; drivers that take the most incredible risks in getting their passengers to their destination. They are brightly coloured, play loud music and have crazy names scrawled on them, like 'Prince Lover Boy' or 'King Road Master'. Matatu drivers drove at incredible speeds and they were responsible for the mowing down of countless pedestrians. Whenever a dense fog descended on the city from the highlands, the matatus were the only ones who did not adjust their speed and they crashed into cars all over Nairobi. As a result the roadsides of Kenya are littered with the rusted remains of crashed vehicles. When the traffic was bad, which was often, they would force new routes over gardens or straight over roundabouts to push to the front. Once I was sat in a traffic jam (or a 'go-slow' as they were called locally) on the way home one evening and I watched a truck driver maneuver his truck to deliberately block some matatus from pushing their way through to the front and making the jam a whole lot worse. In response, the matatu drivers got out of their matatus, pulled the truck driver out of his cab and gave him a good beating. This caused car drivers all around me to get out and rush to the scene. It looked like some were helping with the beating and others were trying to prevent it. And all this happened just a few feet away from the cause of the traffic jam: a broken down truck with the words 'HIGHLY INFLAMMABLE LIQUID' written on the side, where a man squatted underneath, wearing just a pair of shorts and no shoes, holding a lit blowtorch to blast away at the undercarriage of his inflammable liquid load. The whole scene was an impending explosion on so many different levels.

20

Sri Lanka has a bit of a reputation for con-artists and swindlers. Every guidebook I have read warns travellers about a variety of frauds and scams to watch out for. When we first arrived there would be someone at the door every day asking for money: sometimes it would be a personal appeal; a daughter who needed an operation, accompanied by a laminated photo of a sick looking child, or a roof that had blown off, and the rains are coming you know; or a collection for a charity like an orphanage, that does not need clothes or toys, just cash. Sometimes, people would be much more direct and just knock on the door and ask me to give them some money because they had run out. It was often accompanied by wailing and dropping to knees and all sorts of uncomfortable and embarrassing crying and touching of my feet. I was never sure how to handle these callers, what the local protocol was for rejecting them nicely, but Aravinda the landlord told me that I should just 'slam the door in those pesky fellows' faces' which sounded like good advice to me. In any case, I soon noticed that the begging people only knocked on my door and left everyone else in the street alone, so I felt justified in my belief that I was being targeted as a foreigner, and therefore indulged myself in a spot of door slamming.

CULTURE SHOCK AND TIGER BOMBS

Now that we have been here nearly three years, the number of begging callers has dropped significantly. Word must have got around the begging community that I am a hard nosed foreigner. (I am a quarter Scottish after all). Occasionally though another beggar will try his luck. Just this morning a man appeared at the door armed with all sorts of laminated certificates, all in Sinhala, and he informed me in perfect English that his name was Damith and he was my new neighbour. I found this pretty amusing on a juvenile level because his name is pronounced 'Damn-it'. Improbably, he gave me a bunch of bananas, and as I grappled with them he produced the laminated certificates with a flourish and told me that he was collecting money for a big party to raise money for a local children's home. I offered him a cheque, made payable to the children's home but he shook his head, insisted that he could only take cash, muttered under his breath and then pinched back his bananas. Just as I was about to shut the door, he turned round sharply and began shouting at the top of his voice,

'Listen to me. Do not give to any money to these Buddhist people. They are the fraudsters. Especially that one!' and he pointed to the temple at the end of the street where the monk was standing outside as usual.

The monk looked up at the commotion and Damith continued with his rant:

'That one there is a bloody rogue and a boozer' he said and he made a drinking gesture with his hand.

The monk at the end of the street was highly amused and he returned the drinking gesture with a grin and a wave, much to Damith's irritation. I have been thinking about the possible reasoning behind this little scene for most of the day but I am absolutely none the wiser. It will have to go down as another uniquely Sri Lankan moment.

It ranks alongside the time I heard someone singing and playing music in the street outside our house. I looked out the window and saw a strange looking Sri Lankan man with a bugle, a whicker basket and a monkey on a string lead walking up and down our street. While he played music the monkey danced, performed roll-overs, back-flips and a very passable Michael Jackson moonwalk routine. Everyone in the street completely ignored him, so, suddenly he played a different, more haunting tune and the monkey stopped dancing, sat down and watched as a giant cobra wriggled out of the whicker basket and stretched vertically straight, all the time bobbing his head in time to the bugled tune. Still nobody watched him, except for me from the window, so the strange man just stopped what he was doing, waited for the cobra to squeeze back into the basket and then wandered off elsewhere singing his song. Sri Lanka can be a very strange place indeed.

21

If you are obsessive-compulsive, please press 1 repeatedly.
If you are co-dependent, please ask someone to press 2.
If you have multiple personalities, please press 3, 4, 5, and 6.
If you are paranoid-delusional, we know who you are and what you want. Just stay on the line so we can trace the call.
If you are schizophrenic, listen carefully and a little voice will tell you which number to press.
If you are manic-depressive, it doesn't matter which number you press. No one will answer.
If you are anxious, just start pressing numbers at random.
If you are phobic, don't press anything.
A friend of mine at the High Commission in Barbados sent me that in an email and said that I should have it on my answering machine. Although the main part of my job in Bridgetown was visiting British prisoners, or ensuring that Brits who got themselves into trouble were properly represented, an increasingly large part of my job was to deal with the deranged British. Psychiatric cases that went on holiday and got themselves into all sorts of trouble.

When confronted with a mad Brit on the loose, the Barbados police called me. The first time this happened was late at night when the police called me from a south coast hotel to tell me that the proprietor wanted to throw a British man out of his hotel but he had refused to leave. The police said that the British man had glued a number of beer glasses to the bar during the evening and had then hidden under a table and refused to come out. He spent the entire evening down there banging two metal ashtrays together loudly. I told the police that if he was drunk and disorderly then they should arrest him and I would come and see him in the morning. But the police insisted that he had not been drinking and that he was 'a mad man'.

I went to the hotel but I was quite unsure of what I was going to do. I had no idea of how to deal with someone who needed psychiatric help. When I arrived, the man was still under the table, but had thrown the ashtrays away and was now loudly banging two drinks trays together. It was hard not to see the amusing side of things, and the police certainly thought it was funny, laughing out loud at the crazy behaviour. The hotel owner was thoroughly unamused, however, as the Brit under the table had scared off all of his bar customers and he was keeping the hotel guests awake with all the banging.

It turned out that the man was bipolar and had become so relaxed on his holiday that he had decided to go a few days without his medication. As soon as we worked out the problem, he went to the psychiatric hospital, was administered his medicine, made a quick recovery and was sent home.

This was to become a fairly common problem during my three years there and I eventually stopped attending the scene. Instead I contacted the psychiatric hospital and they sent an ambulance to cart them off. There was always a pang of guilt because the Barbados psychiatric hospital, known as Black Rock, seemed somewhat Victorian in its methods. It was an old and rather shabby building and it seemed to overrun with patients and lacking staff. The outer fence was usually lined with patients staring, waving and shouting at passing cars, and on the inside the patients were all on the loose, wandering freely around the hospital grounds.

Like the Barbados Queen Elizabeth hospital, it was very difficult to find the patient you were looking for at Black Rock. The difference at the psychiatric hospital was that while you wandered around and searched for your patient, you were usually followed by a gang of mental patients, all of whom had separate weirdo tendencies. One patient used trot alongside me pointing at my shoes, or my tie, or my pen, asking 'where did you get that?' Another did nothing but walk alongside smiling, quickening his pace if I quickened mine, or slowing right down if I slowed. Another would ask a question and then theatrically look away without waiting for a reply.

A British Rastafarian was arrested at the airport for causing a disruptive scene upon arrival in the country, but the police soon worked out that his problem was of a psychiatric nature and so they sent him to Black Rock. The police said that they had found out that the man was actually on his way to Trinidad, but the airline had insisted he got off at Barbados where he had promptly tried to eat his passport. When I went to see him at Black Rock he was still a bit tetchy.

'Fuck you white boy' was his greeting as I walked into the room. He was sat behind a small table next to a doctor, who smiled and shrugged apologetically at me as I found a seat.

'Ah, that's nice' I said. 'I am from the British High Commission, do you want me to call anyone for you in England, to tell them that you are here?'

'Dogs Cock!' he shouted

'Pardon?' I smiled, it was amusing.

'Monkey shit and balls and fannies' he yelled.

The doctor looked at me and said that he had been like this all day and he was lucky to be in one piece as he had seriously abused the police at the airport and they had been itching to teach him a lesson. Apparently the airline knew he was due to get off in Trinidad but he had been abusing everyone on the plane from halfway across the Atlantic so they were all quite pleased when they managed to get him off the plane in Barbados. The doctor was worried because so far there had been no coherent message out of him all day and they did not have a clue about his next of kin or anyone else to contact on his behalf to find out what his medical condition was. He had eaten the relevant contacts page in his passport.

'Listen, mate' I said. 'You were traveling to Trinidad weren't you? Is there someone there expecting you to arrive? Is there someone there you want me to call to say that you are here in Barbados?'

The man stopped fidgeting with his dreadlocks for a moment and his eyes appeared to light up. There seemed to be a moment of clarity or recollection.

'YES!' he shouted. "YES! You must call them!'

'Who?' the doctor and I asked together, "who shall we call?'

The Rasta jumped up onto the table in one sprightly leap, pulled down his pants to completely expose himself and then held both hands up in the air as he shouted at the top of his voice:

'THE TWELVE TRIBES OF ISRAEL!'

'Ah' said the doctor, 'Do you happen to have a telephone number for the twelve tribes of Israel?'

But the Rasta was ignoring us now, flopping his manhood around in gyrating movements as he danced on the table to a tune of his own devising, heard only by him

22

The President's party is clearly the one with the most money because they have all the really big billboards on all the prominent corners, yet they trumped it all with a huge music and dance extravaganza live on Sri Lankan television that appeared to have been arranged purely to heap praise on the President. The entire Rajapaksa clan was in attendance in the front row and they clapped along as to all the songs and the music. The big finale saw the first performance of a new song, written especially for the night, that (symbolically I presume) told how 'King' Rajapaksa had saved Sri Lanka from the terrorists. The woman singer even suggested that mothers would sing this song to their babies for centuries to come.

As predicted, the Rajapaksa party won the parliamentary election. There are now prominent positions for three of the President's brothers and a new parliamentary seat for another one of his sons. The Rajapaksa dynasty is expanding. If the party wins two thirds of the majority he will have the power to change the constitution and extend his power by more than the current restriction of two terms of presidency and there are lots of rumours around that this is exactly what he is planning. More interestingly, General Fonseca won a place in parliament after campaigning from his prison cell: just as the police removed the monks from outside Fort railway station who were holding a fast to the death in protest of his arrest.

Election day was a public holiday, so we took advantage to finalize our departure date from Sri Lanka and book some tickets online. We are leaving on 6 July and flying to Chicago, where we can then travel onwards to Mary's parents in Wisconsin. We are open to living in most places in the States, wherever the work takes us, but our preference is to stay in Wisconsin. We aim to just rent somewhere and then take it from there.

Therefore, by my reckoning, the light at the end of my tunnel is 88 days away and most of that time will be spent in the monsoon season, which must be coming soon as the heat has reached new levels of unbearable. The last two nights have seen big crackling electric storms with forked lightning streaking across the sky and thunder so loud right above the house that the ceiling lights shudder. I am uncontrollably drawn to these storms, they are so different to anything else I have seen in the world. The storm last night went on for almost five hours and not a single drop of rain fell. I really hope that one of these storms brings some rain with it and then we can feel some relatively cooler weather. We have all passed the point where we can cope much longer with the heat.

23

Aravinda and Amali are driving to the south east of the island to visit Yala National Park, a trip they like to refer to as their Sri Lankan safari. Yala is a safari park of sorts: it is home to elephants, leopards, bears and hundreds of different types of birds, and Aravinda and Amali regularly make the long trip and usually ask us if we would like to accompany them. So far we have always politely declined. For one thing, the trip takes close to seven hours, and for another, the park has been regularly attacked by the Tamil Tigers. Just weeks after we arrived in Sri Lanka, the Tamil Tigers attacked and killed six army soldiers in the park and a seventh soldier was killed in a land mine explosion while trying to escape the attack. Shortly afterwards, the Tamil Tigers attacked and killed a bus load of pilgrims going to the nearby temple in Kataragama. But the main reason we never got excited about the prospect of a trip to Yala was because we had been spoiled by first class safaris when we were in Kenya.

Nairobi was such a violent city that we often packed up our truck and headed out into the bush on safari to get away from it all. The Masai Mara is just over 150 miles from Nairobi although the potholes turn the journey into an all-day affair. The first time we went to the Mara we drove there in our ancient Land Rover with a borrowed tent in search of a campsite. This was in the days before Sam was born, but we did have a couple of kids with us, Connor (10) and Freddie (8) were the children of our friend Maggie, who was visiting us on holiday. Because the trip took longer than we expected, we reached the park at around 3pm, and then we got excited and distracted by sightings of elephants and giraffes and followed the animals instead of heading directly for a campsite. We had a small map of the park with us but it was a Kenya Wildlife Service production and it was next to useless. There were no road signs within the park, in fact, there were hardly any roads to speak of, and the few that were there often ended suddenly or veered off to nowhere. It made navigation somewhat of a challenge, especially when occasionally the route you wanted to take was blocked by a herd of giant buffalo.

The Masai Mara is almost exactly on the equator and so it gets dark quickly at 6pm each night. By 5.30pm we were still looking for a campsite and we were starting to get a little desperate. We had never practiced putting up the borrowed tent we had in the Land Rover and it was looking increasingly likely that we would be pitching the thing in the dark. Everyone else we had seen driving around the park had disappeared back to the safety of their safari lodges, but we seemed to be heading nowhere, and certainly no nearer a campsite.

Just before dusk we noticed a small game ranger's hut in the flat plains and we headed straight for it, hoping to find some rangers inside that could direct us to the Mara River campsite. I was sure that we were close, as I had eliminated all the other tracks on my small map and I could actually see the river at the bottom of the small hill. There were two or three rangers inside the hut, and they told me that the campsite was just the other side of the river, but the only crossing was 40 miles upstream. There was no way we could do it in the dark and we had around 20 minutes of light left.

'Well, where can we put up our tent? We have nowhere else to sleep' I asked.

The Rangers looked unconcerned and one of them pointed over my shoulder to the middle of the grassy plains.

'You can camp out there' he said.

I thought he was taking the piss. 'What? In the middle of the Mara? What about all the animals?' I asked.

The Ranger shrugged and said that people did it all the time, but if we wanted to get to the campsite we had to drive 40 miles north to the bridge and then 40 miles back down the other side of the river.

It was easier than I thought selling the idea to Mary and Maggie, but in truth, what option did we have? We set about making our campsite around half a mile from the ranger hut, because frankly, they were a little strange. They were strange Rangers. As the sun was setting over the plains, we pitched the tent, collected wood and chilled the wine and beers. We cheerfully reassured the kids that all the scary looking animals we had been watching from the safety of the Land Rover all day went to sleep at night so we would be perfectly safe, and as the first flames of the camp fire crackled in the dry Mara wood, we settled down for a nice night under the clear sky and brilliant stars. And how the stars shone. Stars that were not normally visible in the city were shining bright in the sky, and the purple cloud of the Milky Way curled overhead. It was an incredible sight, and one so beautiful that it helped us to temporarily forget the dangerous reality of where we had pitched our tent. It got dark so quickly and so perfectly that the only light we had was from the orange glow of the fire, a circle of maybe three or four metres around us. The lights from the Ranger hut were switched off, and there was no moon. All around us there was nothing but darkness.

And then we heard the first noise. It was not a roar, it was a deep, low, grunting that sounded like it was coming from a large animal, perhaps one that was trotting, and lasted for around

30 seconds before coming to an eerie, slightly echoing end. It was not a noise I had heard before, but instinctively I knew what it was. So did Mary and Maggie, and we all exchanged nervous glances. The two boys were looking at me for some kind of consolation, and I was just about to make up something reassuring, like it must have come from a warthog or something like that, when Mary panicked and jumped out of her camp chair, stood on top of the cooler, and shouted at the top of her voice:

'That - was - a — fuck - ing - lion!'

The kids screamed and panicked and ran to their mother; I gave Mary an admonishing look; and Mary raked around the cool box for the brandy. We decided that we would be fine as long as we kept the fire going, and so we grabbed as much wood as possible from the area immediately surrounding our circle of light. Yet, the wood was so dry that it burnt down quickly and we soon realized that our wood stock was not going to last the whole night.

A couple of minutes after the first grunting, we heard the second one. Thirty seconds or so after that was the third. And so it continued well into the night. No more than five minutes would pass before the grunting would start up again. Sometimes there would be a period of quiet long enough just enough to lull us into falsely thinking that maybe they had left us alone, but every time, they came back. It was so obvious that the noise was from lion; no other animal would have been capable of making the noise, and we had no idea from which direction the noise was coming from. The plains were so large and flat, that sometimes it sounded like the sound was coming from a fair distance behind us, and then moments later it sounded like it could be from very close in front of us. We began to worry that it was a big pride of lions, creeping up on us from all sides.

The adults hit the bottle. We had brought a bottle of wine, a bottle of brandy and a bottle of port to last us three nights of camping, and we cracked them all open and finished them that night. We even skipped our evening meal, which was meant to be sausages roasted on the fire, because we thought the smell of cooking meat would attract the lions. We had cheese sandwiches instead. The booze certainly helped me and Maggie, and Dutch courage kicked in, to the extent that we cursed the lions, shouted at the lions, and eventually toasted the lions with our sloshing glasses of brandy. I smashed up my wooden camp chair to keep the fire going longer and began wandering off in the darkness to relieve myself when ever nature called. No amount of booze could relax Mary though, and to make matters worse, she was convinced that she could see small red eyes peering at her from the darkness.

We all managed to get to sleep at around midnight, after six hours of torment from the lions. The alcohol made us sleep soundly, and I awoke the next morning with one arm stuck out under the bottom of the tent stretched out into the plains. I pulled it back in quickly, half expecting to see it chewed off below the elbow. We all felt a real sense of joyful relief to have survived the night. When we ventured back outside and looked at our site properly in the daylight, we saw that we had pitched the tent between two warthog dens. This had been the reason for all the red eyes that Mary had seen. The warthogs could not get back into their homes, so they stood and stared at us all night. Our relief and laughter was short lived however, as Mary found hundreds of big fat lion paw prints in the sand just a few feet from the campsite. At least we felt vindicated for all our angst the night before.

We cooked sausages for breakfast, throwing the odd one to the warthogs for making them stay out all night. There was no more lion grunting and so we enjoyed our breakfast while admiring the view of a long single file line of zebras and wildebeest making their way right past our tent to the River in the distance behind us.

We decided, unanimously and immediately, that the following two nights of our 'camping trip' would be spent at an expensive safari lodge. We did it for the kids' safety, naturally. We booked into a lodge that morning, and told some of the staff what we had done the night before, and where we had been.

'You stayed at the Musiara swamp' one of the Masai guides told me. 'There are three prides of lions there, all fighting over the land. You put your tent right in the middle of them'.

The experience did not put us off camping in Kenya though, and we got much more professional at it. Mary and I went camping in the Mara again, pitching the tent well away from the nightmares of the Musiara swamp, and in a small wooded vale where Masai warriors would sit outside your tent at a discreet distance and guard your campsite during the night. We would sit outside drinking around the fire until well into the night, playing music and chatting to the young Masai men. We marveled at their pierced and stretched dangling earlobes and purple black skin and they marveled at our CD player boom box. When we put some music on, three of the Masai boys got up and instinctively began dancing in their traditional way of jumping up and down at great heights on the spot, to the sound of Gina G's 'Ooh, Aah…Just a little bit'.

Wherever we camped in Kenya, there was usually someone on hand to volunteer for guard duty for a small fee even though they usually did not inspire as much confidence as a gang of Masai warriors. We always agreed to pay for a guard though, even if he turned out to be a ninety year old man armed with a catapult and a stick. Once, at a campsite by Lake Naivasha, a couple of hours from Nairobi, Mary and I were camping alone in a small field where hippos regularly came out to feed at night. Sure enough, shortly after night fall, an enormous hippo waddled out of the water, looking strangely out of place on the land. The huge beast snorted and farted and ate huge amounts of grass as it edged closer and closer to us, clearly not bothered by us in the slightest and in fact, it seemed to be completely ignoring us. Gradually we relaxed in its presence and eventually as the night wore on, we occasionally forgot it was there until we heard another one of its grunts or snorts.

Suddenly, without any warning, we felt an enormous thundering on the ground and realized immediately that that the hippo was moving around at great pace. We both stood up to watch and before we could react further the beast thundered past, missing us by a matter of inches and sending a guide rope flying and flattening the tent. It moved at such great speed that we felt the rush of wind. Hippos, I know now, can run at something approaching 25 mph over short distances, which is seriously fast. It is the same speed Usain Bolt ran in the Olympics 100m final. Something had obviously spooked it and it had turned and run at full breakneck speed back into the lake. It took the most direct route, and anything in its way was going to be flattened.

It goes without saying that we were seriously unnerved by the hippo suddenly taking off at great speed to the lake and we later learned that many a tourist has been killed by a stampeding hippo. That night, we were buzzing with fright and adrenalin. We knew that we would never sleep with the hippo highly likely to come back out to graze in the vicinity. If it got spooked again there would be nothing to stop him trampling us. We shone our torch into the lake until our fears were confirmed and we saw the hippo coming back out of the water to feed again. I walked up to the campsite reception, hoping to find a guard or someone to ask for help. It was late and everything was locked up, but I found an old askari, the swahili word for guard, leaning against an upturned boat fast asleep. When I walked over he began to stir in an unconvincing attempt to convince me that he had been awake and guarding the camp site the whole time.

'Did you see that hippo?' I asked him.

'Aaah. Hippo. Yes sir' he said slowly, rubbing his eyes.

'It nearly trampled us. We need you to guard our tent'

'I have weapons here, sir' he said, and fished around in his pocket and gave me a small brown paper bag full of stones.

'When the hippo comes back out, you throw these stones and it will go away'. And with that he settled back down against the boat to go to sleep.

I went back to the tent, where Mary was nervously watching the hippo edge closer. She did not calm down any when I told her about the old askari asleep by the boat and his brown paper bag of stones for protection. We watched the hippo get closer and closer and eventually we thought that we should hurl a few stones to see if the old man's plan worked or not. The hippo moved sideways on from us, giving me a large target to aim for, so I picked out a good stone and threw it, with a fairly gentle lob, because I did not want to piss it off. It hit the hippo with a dull thump in the middle of its thick hide and it carried on grazing. I threw another stone, this time a little harder, and the animal turned slowly towards me and gave me a look that seemed to convey that if I tried that again it was going to chew my fucking head off.

I tramped back up to the old askari, who was now fast asleep. After coughing loudly to wake him, I told him that his stones had not worked and so very reluctantly and slowly he followed me down to our tent where the hippo was now munching grass just a few yards away. The old man took a stone out of the paper bag and hurled it at tremendous pace, hitting the hippo square on the side of its jaw. Almost immediately the hippo trotted off away from us and as it moved the old man peppered it with a series of volleys of stones that either hit it on the back of the head or crashed into its side. The hippo did not stop until it was well out of range at least a hundred yards away.

The old man gave a satisfied look. 'My stones work good' he said. 'It is your throwing that not works'.

24

Although we have agreed that we are moving to the USA, and have even set a departure date, Mary still receives emails at work advertising the latest job vacancies with her current employer. We have discussed the possibility of applying for some of them, but I think we are both now committed to a move to the States. The latest advertised jobs are all on the Arabian peninsular, in Kuwait, Oman, Sharjah and Abu Dhabi. They are good jobs, but the thought of living back in the Middle East is wholly unappealing to me, although I must admit, we did have a good time on occasions when we lived there previously.

We lived in Jeddah, in Saudi Arabia, for two years in the nineties, just after the first Gulf War. When we arrived we were struck by how knowledgeable most people were about Scud missiles and whether certain housing districts were within range of Baghdad or not. You needed to know these things when you lived in the Middle East back then.

Jeddah is the second biggest city in Saudi Arabia after the capital Riyadh, and so our mission there was a Consulate-General, not an embassy. There were only eight of us working in the office but such was Jeddah's commercial importance that we had a succession of important visitors to look after. John

Major, Prime Minister, Malcolm Rifkind, Foreign Secretary and Michael Hesseltine, the Trade Secretary at the time, all visited Jeddah, accompanied by top CEOs from British industry's finest, like BP, British Aerospace and Shell. They were all there to make friends and chase the Saudi petro-dollars. Saudi companies employed thousands of Western expats who were all seduced by the big, tax free salaries. The Consulate-General was always cozying up to the families that owned these businesses as they often pushed million dollar contracts Britain's way. One of them was the Saudi Bin Laden Group, a rich family with a notorious renegade son. Osama was merely a fledgling terrorist when we were living in Jeddah, but he was already notorious in and around Jeddah. His brothers were regular guests at the British Consulate, especially when the high profile British ministers and Captains of Industry were visiting. Mary and I met them on numerous occasions, but Osama was never up for discussion. Even by the mid 1990s he had been ostracised by the rest of his family.

Saudi Arabia's sudden oil riches meant that Jeddah changed from a small trading caliphate into a rich modern city almost overnight. By the mid 1990s it was a sprawling city of brand new high rises separated by wide roads and no pavements because it was far too hot to walk anywhere and everyone owned a huge air conditioned car. The only exceptions were the ancient narrow pedestrianised areas of Old Jeddah and the long Corniche road that snaked its way along the Red Sea coast where Saudis often gathered on weekends, (a Thursday and a Friday in Saudi Arabia). Alcohol was strictly illegal so parties on the Corniche usually involved groups of men, drinking tea, smoking hookah water pipes or shishas and performing sword dances. All the men dressed identically and there was no sense of individualism or style. They wore long white ankle length gowns, called a thawb, and a headdress of red chequered or sometimes white cotton on their head, called a ghutra.

Jeddah had all the trappings of a modern city: the amenities, the infrastructure, brand name shops and chains of fast food, and randomly commissioned public art. The city was dominated by enormous roundabouts that showcased crazy and off-beat sculptures: frivolous art that seemed so at odds with Jeddah's strict and conservative nature. One of these roundabouts housed a collection of 29 warships in various states of repose; another had six cars crashing into a concrete block; one had cars driving around a mounted aircraft that used to belong to King Abdul Aziz; and another had a giant mounted bronze clenched fist. It aped a modern city in so many ways, but Saudi Arabia's rapid economic and urban growth had not completely erased the traditional way of life. Until the 1960s most of the Saudi population was nomadic and we often saw families set up a temporary home on the roundabouts, sitting around a camp fire surrounded by modern art with their goats tethered alongside, presumably in reminiscence of when things in their country were quite different.

For the most part, life in Jeddah was a religiously doctrined restrictive experience. Women had a particularly bad time. They were not allowed to drive and not even allowed to go anywhere unless accompanied by a male member of their own family. A group of big stick wielding religious zealots called the Mutaween roamed the streets to ensure that these rules were adhered to. They were employed by an ominously named Saudi government department called the Committee for the Promotion of Virtue and the Prevention of Vice, and their job was to ensure that modesty prevailed, that unrelated men and women did not socialise together and that people were dressed according to Islamic dress codes.

As a foreigner, the biggest risk you had with the Mutaween was over their interpretation of what constituted an acceptable Islamic dress code. This was especially true for women who had to cover up almost completely. For the Mutaween this meant head to toe cover including a face veil, though many Western women objected to having to cover their hair and face. On one occasion, a young Mutaween yielding a stick accosted the wife of the second highest ranked diplomat at the US Embassy. She was dressed respectfully but she had not covered her hair and this had caused outrage with the Mutaween. He prepared to strike the woman with his stick but before he could do so he was knocked out cold by a US Marine who was there as the woman's personal escort. The story became the stuff of legend amongst the Western expats in the city and the woman and the marine became minor celebrities.

Even shop keepers could fall foul of the Mutaween if they did not close their shops at the five scheduled prayer times each day. The call for prayer itself could be a beautiful thing, an exotic chant that floated gently across a warm Arabian evening from hundreds of minarets across the city. On other occasions it was a loud and garishly distorted noise from a broken speaker. The result was the same though: everything in the city closed. The five daily prayers became a real pain to us because their times varied by a few minutes each day and we never adjusted to the new times or we completely forgot about them when we went out. We often got caught in supermarkets when the call for prayer would echo round the building, the lights would all dim and all the staff and most of the customers would disappear off to the nearest mosque. We would just have to wait alone until everyone came back, shuffling around the aisles and talking to other Westerners locked in the shop.

The Mutaween also censored magazines and newspapers in Saudi Arabia before they were allowed on the newstands. The result was that every magazine and newspaper from overseas was blacked out by a marker pen where an article was considered undesirable or a photograph showed too much flesh. Even CD covers were censored. I know I bought my John Lennon Double Fantasy album in Jeddah because there is a thick black marker pen line drawn vertically between the faces of John and Yoko as they kiss on the cover. Videos were also censored. Sometimes they were edited so much that it was difficult to follow the plot. Indiscriminate violence was fine, the Mutaween like that, but an innocent kiss on the cheek or holding hands was deemed immoral and was cut.

Jeddah has always been a trading town, but for most Muslims it is more important because it is the main entry point into Saudi Arabia for the Hajj. Every year, Muslims from all over the world descend on Jeddah to transfer to Mecca, around fifty miles away, to perform a pilgrimage that is sacred in Islam. The Hajj is considered one of the Five Pillars of Islam: the five duties incumbent on all Muslims worldwide. The others, while I am at it here, are a declaration of the oneness of Allah; the commitment to prayer five times a day; fasting during the month of Ramadan; and the giving of alms to the poor. The Hajj consists of a series of rituals that begins with up to three million people walking seven times counter-clockwise around the Ka'bah, a cube shaped granite building covered in a black silk curtain that acts as the centre point and the most sacred site in Islam. Wherever they may be in the world, when a Muslim kneels to pray, it is the Ka'bah that he or she symbolically faces. The Ka'bah houses a black stone that many pilgrims try to kiss, emulating the kiss it received from the Prophet Mohammed. If they cannot kiss it, for three million pilgrims can cause a bit of a crush, they point to it on each of their seven circuits around the Ka'bah. After the Ka'bah, the pilgrims run back and forth seven times between two sets of hills said to be the place where Ibrahim (or Abraham in the Old Testament) was commanded to leave his wife and son in the desert to test his faith. Then they drink from the well of Zamzam, which is said to be the source of the miraculously generated water from God after Ibrahim passed the test. After that they go to the plains of Mount Arafat to stand in vigil and then finally, symbolically throw stones at three pillars called the jamarat in a ritual stoning of the devil. Recently the Saudi Government replaced these pillars with 85 feet long walls because so many pilgrims were missing the pillars with their stones and were hitting people on the others side. Once they have done all that, the pilgrims shave their heads and perform the ritual of an animal sacrifice.

We could not witness this event, other than by watching the 24 hour coverage of it on Saudi TV, because it is forbidden to enter the city of Mecca at any time unless you are a Muslim. There is a bypass road that misses out Mecca if you are a non-Muslim and you happen to be heading that way. It was often referred to as the 'Heathen Highway' by expats and just beyond we could see the road barriers and police that stopped everyone trying to enter Mecca to check to see if they were indeed Muslim. How they check this I do not know. I mean, presumably there is nothing to stop someone like me reading up on Islam and then blagging my way in, pretending to be a Muslim. But of course I never did. You don't take any risks when Islam is concerned.

Before, during and after Hajj, Jeddah was filled with shaved headed pilgrims all dressed in white, speaking a multitude of languages, with hands and faces covered in henna. Many would set up temporary homes alongside the roads in the city and then set up little roadside souks to sell goods from their country to help them fund their passage through Mecca. More alarmingly, lots of pilgrims would sacrifice goats on the roadside a few feet from you as you waited in traffic at a red light, and quite often the city was a swirl of new viruses and sickness as the millions of new arrivals brought all sorts of communicable diseases with them.

Jeddah was the first posting that Mary and I had embarked on together as a married couple. We lived in a guarded compound with access to duty free goods and shipments that were protected by diplomatic immunity. In a country where alcohol and pork was banned, our continual supply of booze and pork chops ensured that we were immediately popular with all the expats in town. Alcohol became a new currency for us. We both trained to become Advanced Scuba divers with an Aussie telephone engineer working for Saudi Telecom as long as we invited him to our place whenever we had a party. We acquired magnificent silk Persian rugs in return for regular invites to the consulate club. We even had use of a beach hut and a share in a jet ski as long as we brought cold beers with us when we visited.

Most expats in Jeddah lived in a compound of some sort, which ranged from under ten houses, (like the British Consulate-General compound) to hundreds of homes (like the enormous Saudia City compound). In our case, the office building was also on our compound, so it meant that I had the shortest commute I am ever likely to have, a walk of a mere fifty yards from door to door. The flip side was that we had to live next door to my work colleagues and the combination of working and living next door to the same people sometimes led to conflict over the slightest issue. Two of our colleagues/neighbours had a stand up fight over the privet hedge about a pet rabbit that kept hopping over and chewing flowers and plants. In most un-diplomatic fashion, one of the protagonists shouted that he would 'nail the fuckin' rabbit to a tree by its bastard ears!'

Paradoxically, it was in Saudi Arabia, the least tolerant and least permissive country imaginable, that we partied and drank the most. As we were the only show in town when it came to alcohol, (for some reason, the US Embassy was far more reticent when it came to getting the expats pissed) we soon learned that it was imperative, to borrow a phrase from Frank Gallagher, 'to know how to throw a good party'. Our compound was a little private universe, immune from the real Saudi Arabia that surrounded us. We had a small bar next to a swimming pool and a big shipping container secured around the back of the office building where we kept hundreds of crates of beer and thousands of bottles of spirits and wines. Every Sunday night was pub night, when we invited over 100 guests to come and drink Strongbow and eat pork scratchings, and we charged them over ten pounds each to drink as much as they wanted, using the proceeds to purchase more booze from the UK. It was a marvellous system to generate goodwill in the British community and make important and useful contacts. The booze was shipped by sea into the country in a diplomatic immunity protected twenty-foot container and it would wait at the port, without the usual search from the Saudi Customs officials, until we could collect it ourselves. There was a common story that everyone knew that recalled the occasion when the Consulate-General received a call from the port to inform us that we had better get down there quick as the 'Ambassador's new piano' was leaking all over the dock.

We threw wildly extravagant parties, inviting hundreds of people and selling tickets at over a hundred pounds each, providing unlimited booze, live music and DJs. We hired a special performances from a troupe of Philipino transvestite dancers, who were 'incredibly dishy ladies' according to the Ambassador the next day in an office meeting, to stifled giggles all round. Even the dreaded QBP (Queen's Birthday Party), which is normally a miserable event and is a staple for every mission all round the world, was a good party in Jeddah. Normally the only people who enjoy the QBP are the embassy's Community Liaison Officer, who revels in her own importance, and the British expat community, who like to come and guzzle as much duty free gin as they can. For the rest of the mission the QBP is usually a lesson in abject misery where no one wants to speak to you unless you are the visa officer, and then you leave with your pocket full of business cards. However the Jeddah QBP always finished up at the poolside bar where people would inevitably end up jumping into the pool in their tuxedos and party gowns, leaving soggy business cards on the bottom of the pool so we always knew the next morning who the rowdiest guests had been.

Sometimes the parties got a little out of hand. On one New Years party we brought in a Scottish bagpiper, shipped in at no cost (as long as we reserved them a table at the party) by

British Airways. The piper stood on the Consulate roof and piped in the New Year to huge raucous cheers below, alerting the Saudi police who needed to be placated with a bottle of Johnny Walker black label. On another occasion during a drinks reception for a visiting ship from the Royal Navy, the randy crew loudly shagged dozens of nurses from the King Fahad hospital in the toilets by the poolside bar. But generally, our hedonistic lifestyle coexisted with the ultra-conservatism of Saudi Arabia because we kept it all in-house, we kept the Saudi's off the rowdy party guest list, and we bribed the Saudi police with the odd bottle of whiskey. I think that we were the last of the 'old school' in Jeddah. As each of our wild colleagues rotated out, he or she was replaced by less frivolous, more no-nonsense career diplomats. This was particularly the case as security issues became increasingly important. This was undoubtedly better for the country, but not nearly as much fun I bet.

25

It recently occurred to me that I have lived overseas for the same amount of time as I lived in the UK. I joined the Foreign Office in 1989 when I was 20 years old, and for the last 20 years I have lived away from home as an expat. It is a neat symmetry and somehow it seems to reaffirm my feeling that it is now time to settle down permanently.

My very first job overseas was what the Foreign Office call 'temporary duty', when they send you overseas to help out an embassy when they are busy. In my case, the embassy was in East Berlin, and they were overrun with work because of the recent fall of the wall. There is only so much a twenty year old with no overseas experience and no German language skills can do, so I was assigned to the Chancery Registry, where papers needed to put away and all the telegrams from London were sent and received. The job was tedious but the chance to live in Berlin at the fall of the wall more than compensated.

It is easy now to forget that just twenty years ago Europe was so politically and culturally divided. West Berlin was a modern city surrounded by a 125-mile-long circular wall. The Berlin Wall, or the Anti-Fascist Protection Wall as it was known if you lived in the East, had divided democratic West Germany from communist, Stasi controlled East Germany for 28 years. Viewed from the East side, there was none of the multicolored peace signs and messages that graffiti covered the Western side of the wall. The Eastern side was smooth white washed concrete and armed guards. I was fascinated by the wall and used to go and stare at it and walk alongside it regularly. It was around 12 feet high with a rounded top, like a high security prison wall. From numerous places in East Berlin you could position yourself so that you had a good view over the wall and into the West, where you could see the flashing lights of clubs and bars, the expensive cars and fashionable people, the restaurants and the shops. West Germans could, if they wished, get a permit and visit the East for the day, but there was no reciprocation. The East Germans could only find a good vantage point and look at the bright lights of the West. For many the temptation was too much and they tried to escape to West Berlin. Estimates vary but most guess that over 5,000 people tried to escape, and that around 200 people lost their lives trying to move from East to West.

When I was there things had already begun to change. The wall was breached in November 1989, when a complicated chain of events led Gunter Schabowski, a spokesperson for the East German politburo, to announce that East Berliners would be allowed to cross the border 'as far as I know, immediately and without delay'. His statement was later presumed to be erroneous, based on rushed discussions that the East German government was having in response to liberation movements in Hungary and Czechoslovakia gathering pace. The remarks were quickly picked up in both East and West Berlin and large numbers of people quickly gathered expectantly at the wall. As East Berliners headed to the checkpoints it soon became clear that none of the guards knew what their orders were and no one would take responsibility for using lethal force to contain the crowds. Eventually the guards opened the gates and East Berliners streamed through to the West. In a celebratory mood, East and West Berliners climbed the Wall and began to dismantle it, and it was all captured live on television.

I arrived in Berlin three months afterwards when the city was in a strange state of limbo. There were clear signs that Germany was on an unstoppable course for reunification and that Berlin would resume its position as capital. Man-sized holes had been punched through the wall in various places and thousands of East Germans had crossed at will through the wall, across no-man's land, and into West Berlin. Yet, you could still not even make a telephone call from the East to the West, or vice versa, because all communications remained barred. Once the initial breach had been made, many East Berliners returned to their homes in the East as they had no where else to go. The East German guards were still armed and at their posts, and made a point of checking documents when people crossed the checkpoints; but similarly, they did nothing to stop people who wanted to bypass the guards and cross through to the west through a hole in the Wall. On a walk around the outskirts of the city one Sunday morning I witnessed the extraordinary scene of East German guards holding up razor wire with their rifles so that an old lady could more easily cross into the west. I even jumped through some of the holes myself, for authenticity and the thrill, but most nights I took a taxi to Checkpoint Charlie and used my Ausweis pass which allowed me to pass freely into the West for a night out.

West Berlin was a great place to be as a twenty-year-old with plenty of money for the first time. I went from carefully watching every penny every month and sharing the rent with six others in North London, to having my own large apartment in Berlin, with all utilities and rent paid, and subsistence payments of fifty pounds a day on top of my salary. That does not sound so extravagant now, but for me in 1990 it was a big deal. I had money to burn. I had a great friend at the embassy called Steve, and we went out most nights to blow away my free daily fifty quid.

CULTURE SHOCK AND TIGER BOMBS

In a way that only twenty-year-olds can manage, we drank in bars and nightclubs every night until the small hours, and then made it in to work on just a couple of hours sleep. Spending the cash in West Berlin was never a problem, it was getting back to the East that caused us problems. Taxi drivers from the West could only drop us off at Checkpoint Charlie, where we would need to walk the hundred or so yards to the East, and then try and flag down an East German taxi to take us the rest of the way home. We would stagger through the checkpoint like seasoned drunks, arms around each other, singing songs, and we did it so often and returned so late each night that the East German guards quickly grew to recognize us. One night, immediately after passing through Checkpoint Charlie and feeling exceptionally reckless, I jumped onto the roof of a nearby Trabant car and then ran along a line of perhaps thirty Trabants all parked in a row, jumping from roof to roof. Trabants were little two stroke 500 cc engine cars and they were the only cars available to East Germans, and they each had a 15 year waiting list. And here I was jumping on their roofs and denting the bodywork of thirty of them in one go. Of course, the noise and laughter of me jumping from roof to roof alerted the guards at the Checkpoint and they came running out of their guard hut to see what was going on. By the time they reached the street I was too far away and so they grabbed Steve, demanding to know my name and where I lived and worked. Steve spoke German fluently and told the guards that he had never seen me before, that we had met that evening for the first time, and that he had no idea what my name was. His actual words were, 'That man is a mystery to me'. The guards had of course, seen us walking past them twice each night for the last three months, but they had no intention of making a big deal out of it, and indeed, the next evening we passed through as usual, with me a little sheepish and the guards all smiles and winks.

Steve was a source of constant amusement. When visiting a West Berlin strip bar where sex change was disturbingly popular, Steve came bolting out of a room to tell me to come and see this 'unbelievable bird with a cock'. In the same place, a short while later, I saw a Filipino girl walking around with Steve's Scotland football shirt on so I asked her where she had got it from. She defensively told me that it was a legitimate swap and it belonged to her now. I reassured her that she could keep the shirt; I just wanted to find the man who had given her it. She pointed into a dark corner of the room where Steve was sitting and laughing on the floor, with a bottle of beer in his hand, dressed in nothing but a thin cotton wraparound skirt. Our stagger through Checkpoint Charlie that night was more eventful than usual, with Steve making friends with all the guards, and at one point getting a piggy back ride off one, all the time dressed in a thin wrap and absolutely nothing else. The guards helped us flag down a taxi in the East, and as soon as we set off, with Steve in the front seat, ('Tak us tae Karl Marx Strasse, big man'), he took off his cotton wrap and waved it out the window like a long pink flag, while sitting completely naked in the front next to the shocked driver.

A few months later, and just before I left Berlin, the same guards helped Steve and I to spray paint our names on the Berlin Wall close to Checkpoint Charlie by holding steady some orange crates we were using as a makeshift ladder so we could spray at the top of the wall. It was an unimaginable change of attitude from guards who were charged with shoot to kill orders only a few months previously. Incredibly, and brilliantly, our names are still there, as the Germans chose to keep that part of the wall when the rest of it was demolished. Our spray painted names are now there for posterity in the Wall museum at the old site of Checkpoint Charlie in Berlin.

Despite the rapidly changing times in Berlin, we were still under orders from the embassy to be careful of Soviet and Stasi approaches for information. Steve and I drank occasionally at a little East Berlin bar at the bottom of the block of flats where he lived on Karl Marx Strasse, even though the embassy still maintained that we should not be out socializing amongst the Communists. We figured that this was out out-dated now, and in any case, we wanted to go to the Eastern bars because the beers were incredibly cheap. I once went to the bar to get us some beers and gave the barman the equivalent of a pound, only to be told that there was not enough money for my change so we could drink for free all night.

The embassy, it turned out, was right to be concerned because one evening Steve and I were approached by some man who wanted to know various things about where we worked and what we did. I cannot give any more details than that, not because of the Official Secrets Act, but because we were both hammered and could not remember much about the man or what he wanted. Nevertheless, we thought we had better report the incident when we got to work the next day and the resident Spooks took it all very seriously indeed. They were itching for any kind of evidence that the Stasi or the KGB were still active. Steve and I were put in separate rooms and asked to describe the man in the bar from the previous evening. When we compared our debriefs later, it turned out the only thing we had agreed upon was that he was buying us drinks and that he was asking us about our jobs. I had described him as a small, bearded man with glasses and Steve had said he was clean-shaven and tall. The political staff at the embassy were quite annoyed with us and told us never to go to the bar again.

Strangely enough, when Steve finally left Berlin around a year after I had moved on to my new posting in Montevideo, his maid confessed to him that she had been employed by the Stasi for the entire time she worked for Steve. She felt it was safe to confess by this point as the Stasi had not contacted her for months and had virtually disbanded. She wanted to tell Steve for honesty's sake. She had made copies of his personal letters, kept track of his comings and goings, made a note of the names of his family, taken copies of personal photographs and anything else that could be used to build up a personal profile. Steve gave her a hug and told her not to worry about it. She was doing what she had been told to do. It was not like she could refuse. In any case, nothing ever came of her reports, apart from perhaps a few outgoing officials at the Stasi HQ having a laugh as they cleared their desks.

26

The rains finally arrived, drenching Colombo with a sustained attack of torrential monsoon rain. It feels a little cooler, thankfully, but now we have rivers of floodwater pouring through open drains and huge lakes on the road full of stranded vehicles. Mary was at the supermarket when the downpour started and when she tried to come back home she found that a huge deep brown lake had formed at the top of our road. It was 100 feet long and 50 feet across and was full of floating plants, tree branches and garbage. The taxi driver refused to drive through it fearing the water was too deep, so Mary was stranded with the groceries unable to get home. She called me at home to come and help her.

I grabbed two umbrellas and three large bags and walked up to the lake, planning to wade through it to collect the groceries and then piggy back Mary through the water. However, the lake was way deeper than I had anticipated. One man trying to pass through had water up to his chest. It also occurred to me that parts of the road here always had an open drain hole, which were always perils to beware of but were now potentially lethal. I had a frightening vision of me disappearing down through one of the holes, never to be seen again.

Luckily, Mr. Green Peas was on hand to provide me with some local guidance. Apparently, by climbing up a wall and walking along a ledge, I could reach a metal grille fence that was part of the cemetery wall where a man-sized hole had been cut by the railway heroin addicts so they could more easily break in to pinch flowers from graves to then sell for a few Rupees. How convenient! I made my way to the hole and then squeezed through into the cemetery, all the while being watched by at least a dozen locals who had gathered to see the street transform itself into a lake. They all seemed to find my antics most amusing, but I guess not too many foreigners crawl along the wall and squeeze into the cemetery through a gap in the fence. The cemetery was on higher ground than the road so the water was only knee high on the cemetery path and I managed to wade through to the far side of the cemetery and find the place where Mary was sheltering in the taxi, because it was still tipping down with rain. We met at the cemetery main entrance and packed the bags with groceries, surrounded by lots of locals who appeared from nowhere but seemed very keen to stand next to us and watch us pack our bags.

There is something quite unnerving about walking through a flooded cemetery; you are never quite sure what, or who, you are stepping on. The water was brown and full of debris, so you really did not have much idea of where your feet were going. We were simply guided by the headstones that popped out of the water like buoys. Suddenly, Mary stopped talking, mid sentence, and jumped nimbly onto a stone plinth that celebrated the life of the deceased Mr. Dudley de Silva.

'SNAKE!' she shouted.

There, just ahead, was a nine foot long snake, swimming quickly in a figure of eight dance towards us. I jumped up next to Mary and we both hugged the tombstone of Dudley de Silva as we watched the huge thing swam right past us. It looked like a cobra and I think there is a good chance that it used to live on the sixth hole of the golf course next door.

27

These days, when considering a new country, Mary and I sit down and check all sorts of facts on the internet and agonize over all the pros and cons. In 1991, when the Foreign Office asked me to complete my postings preference form, I put Montevideo at the top of my list because I liked sound of the name of the city. I liked to say it out loud in a comical Spanish accent 'Mont-ehhh-Veeeeed-ayyoo'. I knew it was in Uruguay, which was South America, and I liked the sound of that too, but I knew nothing about the city or the country. I think I also had Freetown on my list. I did not even know where Freetown was (I know now it is in Sierra Leone, yikes) but at the time I put it down because I thought it sounded cool. Friends of mine did the same thing. I know one guy that got posted to Georgetown in Guyana because his name was George and he thought it would be a laugh. He knew it was somewhere in the Caribbean, but he imagined a small, palm fringed beach with lots of rum punch. It must have come as a bit of a shock when he got there and was surrounded by swamp, mosquitoes and crime.

I know this all sounds shocking now with all the information we have at our fingertips. But back in the late eighties and early nineties, before the internet, information was much more difficult to come by. I remember when we got our first fax machine when I was working in London and I had first joined the Foreign Office. The installation engineer, (for we needed one of those), explained how we could put in a piece of paper, enter a number, and the paper would transmit magically through the air to a different department in Whitehall. We were all astounded; literally speechless at this incredible technology. This is the kind of technological world we lived in back then. Before the days of Google and Wikipedia I was in an information vacuum. Add this to the fact that I was ready for an adventure and did not much care where I was sent to live for the next three years, picking the coolest sounding city name seemed like as good a way as any on my postings preference form. When I got the call from the postings board of the Foreign Office personnel department to offer me congratulations on getting my number one choice, I had to ask the caller to remind me what my number one choice had been. When I called my mum to tell her I was being sent to Montevideo, she wailed down the line, 'Oh no! I knew they would send you to Africa!'

As it happens, Montevideo was nothing like Africa. It was a lovely old city of mostly Italian and Spanish descended immigrants who brought their architecture and culinary skills. The city spread along the River Plate, the wide river that separates Uruguay from Argentina, with a series of apartment complexes alongside La Rambla, a wide boulevard that wound its way along the River Plate for the entire length of city. Getting there was easily the longest trip I had ever undertaken. My flight, indeed the only route back then, involved flying from London to Rio, then connecting to Buenos Aries and then hopping over to Montevideo. It took 27 hours to get there.

I felt cut off from information in way that could never happen in a capital city these days. Our only means of news from the UK was from English newspapers in the Diplomatic bag, which were all three weeks old by the time they arrived. There was no CNN or BBC world news. Everyone had a short wave radio to try and tune in to the BBC world service, but even short wave reception could be a problem. One example involving something dear to my heart, Sunderland football club and football result information. One Saturday night, while all my friends were out in the bars, I stayed in until 9.30pm so that I could listen to the World Service sports roundup to hear Sunderland's result. I knew that if I missed it I would have to wait for three weeks before I found out the score. At 9.30 I listened to all the Sports headlines and then eventually the classified check of the football results with James Alexander Gordon. He began the results, alphabetically through the home teams in each division, and I kept waiting for Sunderland who were at home in Division Two, which meant I had to listen to few results before the one I wanted. The reception was as clear as can be, Liverpool 2, West Ham United 1; Manchester United 1, Tottenham Hotspurs 0; and so on, on to the Second Division, Ipswich Town Wanderers 1, Bristol City 1; Portsmouth 3, Charlton Athletic 0, getting closer, Southend United 0, Middlesbrough 1, we're up next, Sunderland whissssssshsshh (interference) Grimsby Town 1. One little second of interference and it is a three week wait for me to get the football score. It sounds trifling now, but at the time it sent me into apoplexy.

The British embassy in Montevideo was improbably converted from someone's old house and not some specially built fortress like so many are these days. My office used to be some type of back spare bedroom, and the meeting room used to be a dining room. It was quite a bizarre place to work. There were only five British staff there, and around twenty Uruguayans, and we had absolutely nothing to do. My job eventually got cut as someone in London determined that my job was around twenty percent loaded, and I think he was being generous with that. Given all this spare time, I was delighted when my old friend Steve from Berlin said that he would come and out and visit me for a while. At the end of his job in Berlin Steve was offered a new posting to Namibia but he promptly resigned, indignant about the thought of moving to Africa. He later told me that he thought he may have put Windhoek down as his first choice on his postings preference form and then panicked weeks later when he finally got round to looking it up in an atlas. So, after he quit the Foreign Office he came out to visit me in Uruguay. He arrived in early November, at the start of the Uruguayan summer, and when I collected him at the airport I asked him how long he was staying, expecting the usual two or three weeks. But he surprised me by saying that he thought his return ticket was some time in March.

This was good news for me because I was the youngest in the embassy by a good thirty years and I needed someone my own age to get properly plastered with. Steve was a willing and eager accomplice. I often found myself sitting in a nightclub with a large rum and coke at 4am on a Tuesday morning with work in a couple of hours. But all night drinking sessions coupled with a nothing-to-do job and a spare room full of used diplomatic bags that converted nicely into a comfortable siesta bed is a combination that can work.

Our favourite local bar was a whiskey bar, unimaginatively called 'la whiskeria', that served whiskey (clearly), beer and hot dogs, and nothing else. It seemed that whenever we passed, Julio the waiter would run out into the street to coax us in for some drinks, knowing full well that we would offer virtually no resistance. Julio was a scruffy, little, thin man with a permanent three day growth on his chin and a permanent brown stain on his white waiter's jacket. He always dressed the same in his stained shirt and black trousers pulled high up his midriff like a bull fighting matador. He was forever slapping Steve and I on the back and calling us his amigos and he revelled in producing half pint portions of Johnny Walker Red Label, but he hated the girls we took to his bar. On one occasion he tried to throw a female teacher friend of ours out of the bar because she ordered an orange juice. 'Whiskey, Cerveza, Hot Dog, SOLAMENTE!' he yelled at her, frothing at the mouth and pushing her to the exit. Inevitably the girls all hated him, but Steve and I loved it there and so we kept on persuading the girls to give Julio one more chance.

We even took one of ex-Governor of Hong Kong Chris Patton's daughters to the whiskeria once. She was in Uruguay teaching English on a gap year I think, and the old boy's network had ensured that she had a place to stay with the Ambassador until she could sort out her own place. I met her at some official function I was forced to attend and so I invited her out for a few drinks afterwards. I can still remember the look of horror on the Ambassador's face when she crossed over the crowded room to tell him she was going out on the town with me. He shot me a look that clearly indicated that I would be looking for new employment if I misbehaved. We went to la whiskeria with Steve and Mary, who I had just met. I forget which Patton daughter it was now, but it was the one who has a tattoo of an Aztec sun on her backside, because she showed all of us, including a leering and cheering Julio, by standing on a table, pulling down her jeans and bending over. I left the whiskeria episode out of my forced recap of events the next morning when I was cornered by the Ambassador at work.

Although we loved the whiskeria, our favourite place in Montevideo was the Mercado del Puerto, (the Port market) a collection of bars and cheap cafes and restaurants all built in a large old warehouse in the Montevideo port on the River Plate. The cafes grilled the huge steaks that Argentina and Uruguay are famous for and we drank a potent local brew called medio y medio which was half champagne and half white wine. Every Saturday was put aside for an all-day session at the Mercado del Puerto. We met all sorts of people down there. Mary and I once spent the day drinking shots with a dozen self confessed Tupamaros, famous Uruguayan urban guerillas, many of whom were carrying pistols in their belts and all of whom had been imprisoned during the military junta regime in Uruguay. One of the revolutionaries patted his pistol shoved in his belt buckle and promised not to shoot us because it was Christmas Eve, and then roared for more tequila.

Uruguay had only returned to democracy in 1985, just six years before we moved there. The military had ruled the country since the early seventies and groups like the Tupamaros had formed in opposition to an increasingly oppressive dictatorship. The Tupamaros began with Robin Hood style robbing of banks and other businesses and distributing stolen food and money to the poor of Montevideo. However, the military government was enraged by their actions and it imprisoned, tortured and brutally repressed any political dissidents. The Tupamaros responded by turning to violence themselves. They assassinated Dan Mitrione, an FBI agent who had taught techniques in torture in various Latin American countries, and they kidnapped the British ambassador, Sir Geoffrey Jackson, and held him for over eight months before securing a ransom for his release. When the junta was removed, the Tupamaros became a political party and gradually became more influential in Uruguayan politics. The culmination of all this came earlier in 2010 when Jose Mujica, an ex-guerrilla fighter, and who knows, maybe one of our drinking pals back in 1991, won the Presidential election and became the new President of Uruguay.

28

The rains have now fallen, pretty much continuously and with thunder and lightning, for five straight days. Colombo is officially water world. The skies are full and grey and there has been no sunshine to dry up the water. The lake at the end of our street is now well established and even the higher ground in the cemetery is submerged. The only way out of our street is to walk along the railway tracks, which poke out just above the flood line. The main roads are still passable, just, but the buses produce wakes big enough to surf on. Soggy tuc tucs have been abandoned all over the city, and trees have become so laden with water that they have fallen over, roots and all, across roads.

Sam and I have no option but to continue to walk to school as we are trapped by the lake. We can access the golf course along the railway tracks but our normal golf course path is now completely underwater and I have had to carry Sam on my back through water up to my knees, with both of us carrying umbrellas and his school bag. But on the way home I let him get wet and he wades through the large puddles wearing his school uniform.

Mary also walks the railway tracks in the morning now, taking advantage of the only route out, until she can make it to the main road where she can flag down a taxi. She needs to walk a little further on the tracks than we do to reach the main road and she has had a number of close calls with commuter trains that seem to revel in terrifying the increased number of pedestrians on their track. But at least Mary can make it to work, which has not been the case for all of her colleagues. One of them, Aaron, who lives a little further out of town in a house by a labyrinth of streams and rivers has been completely trapped in his house since the monsoon started. Aaron's boss, a Brit, unaware of the local realities, told Aaron to put on a pair of shorts and wade through the water and get to work. If everyone else was making it through the floods then so should he. In response, Aaron sent in a series of photographs of the view outside his home with crocodiles bobbing in the waters outside his front gate.

While not as life threatening where we live, the rains have brought added health problems to our household. The house is soaked right through and smells of mildew and mold and the constant damp seems to have increased our susceptibility to viruses and bacteria. We have all developed stomach pains and diarrhea, Mary has an awful ear infection and I have a boil the size of a baseball under my armpit. There have been power cuts all over the city and many people have been flooded out of their house. Kunty called us to say that she was underwater, and on local radio this morning I heard the weather report say, in a classic case of understatement, that 'over 11,000 people had been affected by the inclement weather'. The radio went on to reassure listeners that the 'rains would continue until they stop' and that the weather would soon 'improve to normal monsoon conditions'.

On top of my discomfort because of the large boil, my mood has been sorely tested because the rains have stopped the reception on our satellite TV and our internet connection has vanished. For the first time in 35 years England won a cricket tournament and I missed the winning runs because a downpour at the critical moment fuzzed out our television signal.

The newspaper this morning said that the Victory Parade due to be held this week on Galle Face Green had been postponed because of the inclement weather. (There is that that word again, inclement; can it not be called what it is? Stormy, unpleasant, foul, nasty, wild, severe, extreme?) It dawned on me that it is almost exactly one year since the end of the war. There was a big Victory Parade last year, which I thought was a bit inappropriate seeing as Colombo is also home to tens of thousands of Tamils, but I could see why it may be important to recognize the sacrifices of the Army and to give them their moment of glory. Yet now it seems that this is going to be an annual event, (inclement weather permitting). How can a yearly Victory Parade be in the best interests of national unity? Where is the desire to move on from what happened and integrate people, religions, culture and language? Could there even be a more divisive issue? Surely the first thing Sri Lanka needs to do if it is serious about fostering integration and harmony is to stop these Victory Parades. Why not introduce a Reconciliation Day that celebrates all the peoples of the country?

29

One major irritation in Colombo for Sam and me is that there is nowhere for us to kick a football around. We play in the street sometimes, but it is not a big enough area for us to play properly. We could try and clear some space on the beach near Mount Lavinia, but it is really crowded there and we would get mobbed by locals wanting to join in or sell us stuff. I have always found that people here are usually genuine and friendly, but they are also incredibly invasive. Sometimes it would be nice to go about your business without the drama that follows you around in Colombo. It would be nice to blend in and be one of the crowd, to be able to go to a shop without a beggar following me in and repeatedly tugging my sleeve, or to be able to go for a walk without tuc-tuc drivers stopping in front of me and hassling me to get in, or to have a kick about with my son without the attention of dozens of curious Sri Lankan onlookers. The reality of life for us here is that we stand out.

There is a large park in the centre of Colombo called the Vihara Mahadevi Park which has plenty of grassy areas that would be ideal for football if we could cope with the interruptions. However, the park has an additional problem, it is completely overrun with young couples snogging and fondling each other in the bushes and behind trees. I have nothing against that, let young love flourish, but the sheer huge scale of it means that the park is actually quite an uncomfortable place to visit. I was under the impression that Sri Lanka was a conservative society, so the breast fondling and crotch grabbing that I saw in the park came as a surprise. But this morning I saw in the news that the police in Kurunegala and in Matara, two large towns in Sri Lanka, have arrested over 500 couples this week and charged them with indecent behaviour for their snogging and fondling sessions in parks in the respective towns. I wonder if they are planning a raid in Colombo? They will catch thousands in Vihara Mahadevi Park.

Thinking of all these young couples in love has reminded me of Montevideo again. The Mercado del Puerto is where I met Mary for the first time, and it is also the place where Steve and I first met Natasha. We were at Roldo's bar, tucking into bottles of medio y medio, when Natasha and her friend Gabby came over to talk to us. They were eighteen years old and dressed in their school uniforms and Steve was all drool and lechery. They told us that they had to complete a school English assignment and so they would like to practice their English skills with us. It turned out that they could barely speak English, and of course we spoke no Spanish, but we had a nice afternoon and Steve swapped telephone numbers at the end of the day. I did not think we would see the girls again, but Steve seemed consumed with them and arranged for us all to meet up the next day. I told him that I did not want to go, I had recently met Mary and was itching to go out with her instead. Steve pleaded with me, insisting that I could take first pick, he liked Natasha and Gabby equally, he would take either one. I was resolute however and so Steve went off to meet both the girls alone, in a bit of a huff with me.

Later that evening when he got home he said that he had spent the evening weighing up the pros and cons of both Natasha and Gabby and that on balance, he preferred Natasha, although it was a close call. He placated Gabby by telling her that I was gay, which she apparently accepted without question or surprise. Steve arranged to take Natasha to the New Years Eve party at the whiskeria, which we were all going to. Julio had extravagantly brought in some flashing lights for the bar and he was considering a DJ so he could do some of his dance moves. We were all looking forward to it, even the girls.

Steve and Natasha spent the whole evening together, then New Year's Day, then most of the following weeks which was the middle of the Uruguayan summer. We spent hours at Pocitos beach which was close to my flat, or over to Mary's where there was a swimming pool. I finished work at 1pm because under Uruguayan law, summer hours were 8am to 1pm. Natasha was an ever-present at my house for all this time, and she and Steve were getting closer and closer. But, by the middle of January Steve was getting more and more frustrated. He confided to me that Natasha was a good Catholic girl and she would not give in to his carnal desires. I laughed and told him that the only way he was going to get into Natasha's knickers was if he married her. Steve nodded his head, apparently contemplating the idea. I gave him an admonishing look and a little pep talk to try and knock some sense into him. Then I left for work, with Steve alone at home for once, with time for him to mull over the the conundrum of celibacy or marriage. I reckoned that he would soon come to his senses, and when I came back from work I half expected Steve to announce he was going to see less of Natasha from now on. But no. When I opened the door, Steve and Natasha were waiting for me with big smiles and even bigger news. They were getting married at the end of January. Just six weeks after they first met.

The wedding in Montevideo was actually a great success. Once everyone had realized that they were serious about the whole thing, even though they could still barely communicate with each other, plans went underway for the party. After a couple of days it dawned on Steve that there were people back home in Scotland that he had better tell about his upcoming wedding. He asked me if he could use my telephone to call his parents. I reminded him that this was going to come as a huge shock to them; their only son marrying a Uruguayan girl that he has just met, so he had better break the news easy. Steve was very relaxed about it all, and did not expect any problems: 'Oh aye, big man, I know, nae bother'

He picked up the phone to dial and I sat down next to him to listen how Steve was going to tell of this upcoming epic moment of his life to his parents thousands of mile away. I heard his mum pick up the phone in faraway Glasgow, and then Steve shout down the line:

'Ma! It's me, Stevie. You'll never guess, am getting married to a Uruguayan!'

Nice one, Steve. Way to break the news gently. I went into the kitchen to make a cup of tea and came back five minutes later to hear Steve's dad yell down the line, 'What do ye mean you know what you're fuckin' doing?' So, I went off to the whiskeria to give Steve some private time on the phone.

I am pretty sure the conversation did not go as Steve had planned it, but as far as he was concerned only one thing mattered and he was determined to go ahead with the wedding. What he did not know was that I got a call at 3am a couple of days later from Steve's mum who said that they had been thinking, and that if Steve was going to get married, then they wanted to be there to see it. We agreed that I would collect them from the airport and put them up for a few days, keeping the whole thing secret so to surprise Steve. When the day came, Mary held a BBQ at her house and using the excuse that we were low on ice, we headed off to the airport to get Alan and Mary, Steve's parents. We returned to the party and watched Steve and Natasha dancing, oblivious, by the side of the pool, until, gradually they turned round and Steve caught a glimpse of his parents. He went white with shock but elation soon took over. Natasha on the other hand passed out on the lawn and had to be coaxed back to consciousness with a wet cold flannel before she could meet the new in-laws for the first time.

On the wedding day Steve and his dad wore kilts, which was a novelty in Uruguay, and hugely entertaining to Julio, who had agreed to provide cut price drinks for all the wedding guests at the whiskeria. For months afterwards, even when he knew Steve had left Uruguay with his new wife, he always asked me in a fit of giggles if I was missing my 'friend in the big red skirt'. The British ambassador was from Aberdeen and in a moment of Scottish brotherly love he agreed to wish Steve and Natasha all the best with a little speech at the wedding. He and his wife came along and had a grand old time along with the rest of us.

It was unusual for me to be in the same place as the ambassador and having a good time, because, more usually he was looking for ways to discipline me as I seemed thoroughly adept at pissing him off. Much of it was down to sheer indifference on my behalf. Because there was no actual work to do in the office I got used to doing nothing and quite resented it when the Ambassador dreamed up something to keep me occupied. Once, when he called me up and asked me to come into his office, I replied, without thinking it through properly that he would have to wait because I had just lit up a cigarette. His suspicions were aroused when, on an uncustomary exploration around the office, he discovered my bed of diplomatic bags although thankfully I was not taking a siesta at the time. Sometime afterwards he worked himself into a real temper because he wasted all afternoon looking for me while I was sunbathing on the embassy roof, radio on, in the summer sunshine, pretending to fix a satellite dish. When he eventually found me I avoided any serious trouble because I talked authoritatively about how vital the satellite dish was to the embassy communication system. But the ambassador strongly suspected the truth: which was that I had no clue what the dish did, never mind how it operated. On another occasion I left him stranded outside the embassy early one Monday morning waiting for me to turn up and open the combination locks (in the days before mobile phones, so he could not contact me) because I visited Buenos Aires for the weekend and deliberately missed the last ferry back because I had learnt that Pavarotti was performing a big, free open air concert later on the Sunday evening and decided on the spur of the moment that Pavarotti was more important than going to work. I did a similar thing a few months later when I got stranded in Brazil, although that time it was not my fault. That did not wash with the ambassador though and coming back late from Brazil was one indiscretion too many as far as he was concerned. He flipped his ambassadorial lid and wrote a long letter of complaint about me to the Personnel department in London. (But in true Foreign Office fashion, it was all put down to a personality clash with no lasting damage).

The trip to Brazil was legitimately not my fault. Honestly. Mary and I booked an 18 hour bus ride, all the way through Uruguay and into southern Brazil to Florianopolis, an island tourist resort. We stayed a week, enjoyed the sun and sea and drank dozens of caipirinhas, Brazil's national cocktail made of the rum-like cachaca and mixed with sugar and lime. We rented an old VW Beetle car and drove around the surrounding area. We visited a small town with a German name in the middle of Brazil called Blumenau. It had Bavarian style architecture and restaurant menus full of sauerkraut and schnitzel. Apparently there was an unusual influx of a particular type of German immigrant there shortly after the Second World War. The type of immigrant Simon Wiesenthal was always interested in. The town was full of blonde hair and blue eyes.

On our last night in Florianopolis we used up all of our Brazilian currency on food and drink and any little piece of toy junk that people were selling in the streets. We figured that if we were getting on the bus again early in the morning then we would not be stopping again until we were into Uruguay and so we may as well spend all our Brazilian money. Mary bought paper windmills and curly straws and a flashing light yoyo, and

I spent all my money on an excellent fake gun that fired caps with an impressive bang. So, when we turned up for the bus early on a Sunday morning, with nothing but a few coins in our pockets, we were shocked to be told by the driver that there were no seats available for the return trip to Montevideo. We checked our tickets again, and we had the correct date, but the bus had been overbooked and the driver shrugged, told us we would have to catch the bus that left next Sunday (a whole week away!) and drove off without us.

We stood there in incredulous silence with our bags and no money. We did have a credit card but we needed cash, and like everything else in Brazil on a Sunday, all the banks were closed. In effect, we were penniless. We tried a bit of hitchhiking, but after an hour of so of standing in the sun without success, we both wanted to try something else. The sheer distance made it highly unlikely that hitching a ride would work anyway. It was like standing outside the Colosseum in Rome on a Sunday morning looking to hitch a ride back to London to start work the following morning. We decided to head for Florianopolis airport in the hope that we might charge a flight to Uruguay on our credit card. We returned to our guest house, where we had stayed for the last week, and we successfully begged the owner to give us a lift to the airport in the back of his pickup truck. Florianopolis had a very small provincial airport and there were no flights to Uruguay, but they did have one daily morning flight to Porto Alegre (or 'happy harbour' as it translates to in English) which was south and at least it was heading in the right direction.

We landed at around midday at Salgado Filho International Airport in Porto Alegre and discovered that we had just missed the one flight to Uruguay. There were only three more flights out of Porto Alegre that day: one to Rio de Janeiro (wrong direction), one to Brazilia (definitely the wrong direction) and a final flight at 9pm to Buenos Aires. The flight to Argentina was our only option. If we got to Buenos Aires there was always a good chance of getting a connecting flight to Montevideo, although we would not arrive in Buenos Aires until close to midnight, and neither of us thought that flights operated during the night. Still, we had no choice, and we charged more flights on our credit card and booked a flight to Buenos Aires.

By this stage we were both really hungry. We had expected to be fed on the bus, and so we had brought nothing more than a bag of crisps and some sweets that were to be snacks. We noticed a small bank open at the airport and tried to get some money out on our card so that we could buy some food. However, the bank would not advance cash on our foreign credit card. Sensing that Mary and I were close to tears at this point, the bank teller gave us 10 Cruzeiros for food. We thanked him profusely and asked for his address so we could repay him the money by post from Uruguay, but he waved us away dismissively, saying that the money was 'nothing' and that it was 'sheeeet'. Nevertheless, it was enough for us to share a sandwich and a bottle of water at the small café that serviced the airport. We sat on the hard metal seats, in the dull airport, nursing our bottle of water for seven and a half hours listening to announcement after announcement in Portuguese before our flight was called. We checked in and entered the duty free area where to our total delight there was a duty free shop that was willing to accept our credit card. We bought the only sustenance that was available, bottles of Grolsch and Toblerone, and drank and ate greedily in the departure lounge ignoring the strange looks from our fellow passengers.

After a three hour flight to Buenos Aires we landed at Ezeiza airport, only to confirm our worst fears that there were no flights to Uruguay until 9 am the following morning. We both needed to be at work for 8 am, and this flight would mean we would be at least three or four hours late. I knew I was already on a last warning after the Pavarotti incident. An information officer at Ezeiza airport told us that we might be able to get an earlier plane if we tried at the smaller provincial airport called the Aeroparque Jorge Newbery, so with nothing to lose but money we jumped on another bus, using the credit card again, to try at the other airport. A two hour round trip confirmed that there were no flights to Montevideo from the smaller airport and that our only option was to book seats on the 9 am flight from Ezeiza. At 2 am, Mary and I booked our flights, accepted that we would be late and therefore in trouble at work again, and looked for somewhere to sleep on the floor of the airport. Mary slept on some seats, but I found it more comfortable on the floor. I was so tired at this point that I did not mind that that floor was that strange rubber material of semicircular mounds designed to provide a better grip underfoot. It left me with strange round red craters all over my face when I woke up a few hours later.

At 8am, twenty four hours after starting off in Florianopolis, we finally got ready to fly to Montevideo. We both checked in with good spirits, I was ready for the Ambassador rant, ready to relate the story of how I had tried my hardest and spent hundreds of pounds on my credit card to get back in time and that it was hardly my fault that South America was so unreliable. I smiled at the security guards and put my small fabric bag on the X-Ray machine and walked through the metal detector. As I waited absentmindedly at the other side of the machine watching Mary go through her security routine, I was suddenly and violently pushed against the wall and surrounded by four or five Argentine soldiers who all cocked their automatic weapons and held them to my head. They shouted all at once, unintelligibly, prodding their guns and pointing at the X-Ray machine screen at the image of my bag. And there, smack in the middle, as clear as day, was the unmistakable image of my metal toy cap gun, bought with my last pennies in Florianopolis. 'You. Terrorist!' shouted one of the guards. 'No' I shouted back nervously, and in an attempt to show them that it was a toy, fished the toy gun out of my bag and held it aloft. I was tackled to the floor immediately and it was only after four of the soldiers had pinned me to the ground for ten minutes, all the while at gun point in full view of everyone else boarding the plane, that the soldier in charge declared it a toy and gave it back to me. I sheepishly took my place on the plane home amongst my grinning fellow passengers, where Mary was laughing and pointing out she was traveling with a Revolutionary.

30

We had fourteen consecutive days of non-stop rain in Colombo. Non-stop, constant, heavy monsoon rains. There seemed to be no end. The sheer force of water began to freak me out. Water is everywhere. Our roof is leaking, water is seeping through the windows, the house smells of damp: damp wood, damp carpets and damp clothes; the fungus is taking over the bathroom ceiling, all the wooden doors and window frames are jamming because they have expanded with moisture and the roof and windows regularly shake because of the severity of the cracking thunder. I cannot believe that a couple of weeks ago I was complaining about the sun and I was actively looking forward to this. To top it all, the TV has hardly worked for the last two weeks because the satellite signal has been permanently lost in the clouds and rain.

I have been completely housebound because of the weather, apart from carrying Sam to school through knee-high pools of water on the golf course. Spending so much time inside would not be good for me under any circumstances, but it has been made worse because my stomach pains and diarrhea got worse, I developed a fever of 40 degrees centigrade and could not get out of bed. And all the time, the boil under my arm continued to grow and fester and sting. I had to drag myself to see a doctor and he said that I had a bad case of gastroenteritis, but since I had had diarrhea for over five days, I was close to being hospitalized and put on a drip. I have been recovering over the last couple of days, although I have lost an alarming amount of weight. My stomach has now dropped to secondary illness behind the huge boil, which has started to ooze thick yellow and green slime all over my armpit. Thankfully the pain of the boil has reduced now that it has burst, but the poisonous slime it is pushing out into my underarm hair has ruined any possibility of maintaining even a minimum level of personal hygiene. I am a completely hideous mess.

But some good news: my parents got that DVD parcel I sent. Sri Lankan Noel Edmonds at the post office must have been compelled for some reason to try and act in the best interests of the customer. And finally, the sun is attempting to break through the thick blanket of cloud and have a go at evaporating away some of those floods.

It is Wesak, which is often interpreted as 'Buddha's birthday' in the west, although technically Wesak encompasses the birth, the enlightenment (Nirvana) and the death of Buddha so it is more like Christmas and Easter rolled into one. Sri Lanka celebrates Wesak by hanging Buddhist flags everywhere. Why Buddhism has its own flag, I cannot imagine, but at Wesak the blue, yellow, red, white and orange striped flag can be seen everywhere. It hangs from tuc-tucs, taxis, cars, buses and trucks, and it hangs from houses and is draped across streets and busy junctions alike. Wesak is also the time when lanterns are hung all over the city. Houses hang them outside their doors, businesses hang huge ones outside their offices, children make them at school, and the city devotes an entire street, Bauddaloka Mawatha, to the display of public lanterns, covered in protective plastic wrapping in case it rains. In addition to all the lanterns, there are also huge 100 foot high pandols dotted around the city in strategic locations. The pandols are bizarre and enormous contraptions which look like they have been taken from travelling fairgrounds. They depict, in flashing lights and loud crashes and bangs and music, scenes from the 550 stories of the past lives of the reincarnated Buddha. Hundreds of people gather in front of them to watch gaudy reenactments of their favourite Buddha stories using painted cut out figures of the Buddha moving crankily around cheap looking story boards. Wesak is very much a community event and multiple feeding stations suddenly appear all over the city, built from scaffolding with canvas walls, where people pool resources and provide curry and rice for the needy for the two days of the Wesak celebration.

Our street has got in the Wesak mood and someone has strung thousands of twinkling lights, like the small ones we put on Christmas tress, from lamp post to lamp post. Thinly shredded multicoloured plastic ribbons hang from all the telephone lines that crisscross the road. It looks very nice I have to say. They have also set up a big feeding station with free curry and rice, and Mr Green Peas and the railroad boys have virtually moved in there permanently, along with most of the Borella station police. Someone on a loud microphone at the temple is singing songs, reciting long stories in Sinhala and banging drums and crashing cymbals. There was a big whip round to pay for all this, and two young collection boys came knocking on our door just as Mary and I were returning from a trip out on our scooter. They waited for us to dismount and then held out their hands and asked Mary for some money. She asked me if I had some cash for Wesak, and so I gave them 200 Rupees. It was all I had in my pocket; it is around two US dollars. They were clearly expecting more and they intimated that I should pay more because I was a foreigner. I was irked that they were not satisfied with the 200 Rupees so I said they could give me it back if they were not happy with the donation. One of the collectors gave me a disapproving look, so I told him, 'Look mate, I couldn't give a fuck about Wesak' and ended up getting a kick in the shins from my wife.

We booked into the Mount Lavinia hotel for one night, to get away from the loudspeaker at the temple, which is a 24-hour deal at Wesak. We did it to escape the noise, but also to treat ourselves to some comfort after the months of stifling heat and then the floods and illness. We wanted to enjoy a room cooled by an air conditioner and take a long hot shower in a bathroom without fungus on the ceiling. The Mount Lavinia hotel is a beautiful old building on the southern outskirts of Colombo, occupying a prominent position overlooking the beach. It has a grand entrance with a beautiful fountain where men with funny feathered hats, dressed in old fashioned pressed white shorts and knee high socks open the door for you when you arrive. The hotel was once the grand residence of Sir Thomas Maitland, an ex-governor of Sri Lanka in the days when it was still called Ceylon. Legend has it that as he was building the mansion he fell in love with a local girl and had a tunnel built between her house and his wine cellar so they could meet in secret. The girl's name was Lovina, and the hotel and indeed the whole suburb of Colombo that surrounds it has been called Mount Lavinia after her ever since. You can see the hotel in the movie 'The Bridge on the River Kwai'; it was used as the location of the hospital where William Holden was recuperating after his escape from the Japanese prisoner of war camp.

Our plan was to pamper ourselves and to gorge on the three buffet meals that our full-board package deal allowed. Yet, even in places like this, Wesak invades. There was no alcohol allowed and our three buffets were completely vegetarian. I had assumed that the hotel would make some exception for their fee paying guests and allow them some meat and booze if they so desired. It irritated me to such an extent that I ended up getting a 45 minute taxi ride back to our house so that I could bring back a bottle of rum. I had to smuggle it into our room in a brown paper bag. It was like being back in Saudi Arabia for christ sakes.

31

When we move to America I will need to apply for a 'green card' so that I am allowed to work, for alas, I fear I will have to work when we go there. Even though Mary and I have been married for nearly 20 years, she was born in the States and our son has an American passport, I will still need to go through the bureaucratic process of becoming a 'legal alien'. It appears that I will need to provide a 'police certificate of good conduct' from everywhere I have lived for more than a year. That means I will need to deal with the respective police forces of Cote d'Ivoire, Saudi Arabia, Kenya, Uruguay and Barbados. You know, I think that it may not be a straightforward task. My plan therefore is to give the US Authorities my address in England for the period I was employed by the Foreign Office, thereby conveniently removing the requirement of a police certificate from the countries I lived in while I was in the Diplomatic Service. Crown servants technically reside in the UK, anyway. That narrows the list down to a police certificate from two countries only: the UK and Sri Lanka. The UK one I have already applied for on-line. The Sri Lankan one required a visit to my local police station.

Borella junction is the name given to an ugly collection of shops built around the intersection of three busy roads. Buses collect passengers here, so it is always full of conductors shouting destinations, drivers blasting their horns and other vehicles trying to maneuver around the buses and avoid the jaywalkers. There is a three story concrete building that houses an indoor market and a few sports shops full of cheap cricket equipment and poor copies of Manchester United and Chelsea football shirts. On the street outside, people lay out goods for sale on mats on the floor: cheap battery operated toys from China; cheap T-shirts proclaiming their owners to be a 'Sexy Lady' or a 'Lover Boy'; or tennis racquet shaped mosquito killers with electric wires where the strings should be so you can waft and fry flying insects. It is a noisy, dirty part of town where life is one long push and shove, full of suspect characters and petty crime, which makes it, I suppose, an entirely appropriate place for the local police station.

The first thing you notice about Borella police station is how tatty it is. It is all peeling paint and rain stained walls. The windows have no glass in them and the shutters are held up with bits of string or sticks fashioned from fallen branches from the trees in the forecourt. There is nothing to indicate that the building is Borella police station: it was only some sustained questioning of pedestrians around Borella junction that led me to the place, tucked away in little side street behind the bus station and the post office where I had the trouble with the DVDs.

The second thing you notice is how many police officers are hanging around doing nothing. There were at least a dozen sitting in the shade in the dust under the trees with their shoes off and there were many more sitting on plastic seats on the large verandah on the front of the building. There was no obvious entrance that I could see, but I did notice a very large lady in an ill-fitting police uniform who smiled and giggled when I asked her where I might get a police certificate of good conduct. She replied in a long sustained burst of Sinhala, which led to a bizarre five minute conversation in which neither of us could understand a word the other said. Another police officer sitting nearby eventually stood up and told me in English to follow him. I was shown through to a tiny office where a sergeant was sitting at a desk reading a newspaper with his big dusty boots on the table and his uniform shirt open at the front revealing his big belly. He may have given an unconvincing first impression but he at least knew what I was asking for. I could barely hear him as he spoke quietly in faltering English in front of a big framed photograph of Rajapaksa, underneath a ceiling fan that sounded like it was about to take off with the roof, but the gist of the conversation was that I needed to return with a copy of my passport, a copy of the permission paper that allowed me to live at my home, a letter from my landlord that confirmed that I was allowed to live at my home, and a copy of my visa to show that I was legal in Sri Lanka. After that, I could have the letter I needed.

By Sri Lankan standards that was a breeze. I returned home and got what I needed. I whipped up a letter for Amali to sign, and she stopped berating the new maid just long enough for her to sign my letter. 'These people need to be trained' she told me as I backed away thanking her for the signature.

I returned to the police station less than an hour after I had spoken to the big bellied sergeant, but when I got there he had gone and the rest of the police there denied that there had ever been a sergeant there at all. I went back to the large lady in the ill-fitting uniform but all she could do was giggle at me. Convinced that the whole staff were playing some kind of childish game with me, I decided to wander about the station opening doors, looking for someone who might help. I found another little office, this time with four uniformed police officers all crowded around one desk underneath another one of those large framed Rajapaksa photographs and a loud ceiling fan. Their desk was full of paper: statements, books, newspapers; and they all had large round heavy stones on them to stop them from being blown around the room by the industrial sized fan. For all that wind, it was still stifling inside.

I tried to explain what I wanted again, and was encouraged to learn that the oldest officer spoke a little English.

'I need a police certificate of good conduct' I said.

'You need a police certificate' the policeman replied.

'Yes correct' I nodded enthusiastically, encouraged that maybe there was some common understanding.

'Correct' he repeated.

'I need it for migration purposes, to go to the USA'

'The USA' he said, looking more perplexed now.

'That's right'

'That's right' he said, beginning to frown.

I realised that he was just repeating everything I said. He probably did not understand a word I was saying. I smiled and asked him slowly if he could help me.

'You are from?' he said, changing the subject dramatically.

'I am from England' I said

'Ah, England. You go to England'

'No. I am going to the USA'

'Not England?'

'No, I need a letter from the Sri Lanka police to go to the USA'

'Ah, you need letter to go to the USA'

'YES' (I felt encouraged now, we were getting somewhere). 'I need a letter from you to say that I have not been in any trouble here in Sri Lanka, I have a clean record'

'You live in Sri Lanka how long?' he said

'Three years'

'Ah, how is Sri Lanka?'

'Sri Lanka is a very nice place. I like it very much'

'You have family?' he asked

And so it went, we had a ten minute interlude where we talked about my family and Sri Lanka, and we deviated well away from where I wanted the conversation to be.

Eventually the old police man told me to take a seat, he spoke to his three colleagues in Sinhalese and then they all promptly filed outside. I sat in the dark office alone for five minutes until they wandered in again, one by one, looking at me. A different policeman started to speak this time, asking the same questions as the old man. Patiently, I went over the same answers as before, namely that I was from England, that my family lived here in Borella and we had been here for three years.

'Look, I need a police certificate' I said, trying desperately to get back the conversation back on track.

'A cert-if-ic-ate' the policeman slowly rolled the syllables around as he repeated me, but he clearly had no idea what I had said.

'A letter from the police?' I tried again.

But the four of them all started talking in Sinhala again, and I looked at them all blankly. I began to think that the certificate was not going to happen, and that even if I did manage to make myself understood, then the actual certificate would be in Sinhala and completely useless for my purposes.

A succession of other people came in with their various problems and the office became crowded as statements were written down. I gave up my seat for an old woman and ended up being shunted onto a pile of sturdy boxes full of old records and files. The police officers dealt with the various visitors, occasionally looking up at me and repeating a question they had already asked:

'You are from?' 'I am from England'

'You need to go to England?' 'No, the USA'

'You from the USA?' 'NO'

Every once and a while, without warning, one of the policemen would leave the office and not return for around ten minutes, and when they came back, they would ask me again what I wanted, and again I would try to explain. After an hour of this, one of them walked in carrying a pad of forms with 'Police

Station — Borella — Police Clearance Certificate' written in English in capital letters across the top. All that was required was for them to fill in my name and passport number and to stamp the bottom of the form and it was done. I swear I could not have been more surprised. The oldest policeman copied my name from my passport, repeating the names out loud as he wrote, (Meester…Harrrrry…Marcus….) and completed the form. Then he did it again, and then again, so he could give me one copy, keep one for himself, and then put another copy in some file that he took a good fifteen minutes to fish out of the filing cabinet behind the boxes I had previously been using as a seat.

'You now give me 250 rupees' he said, which I willingly handed over (and was not offered a receipt for incidentally) and I left the police station in good spirits surprised that my trip had been a fruitful one. I even wished the fat policewoman on the verandah a happy Wesak. She giggled.

32

We have just over a month left in Sri Lanka: the 6th of July has been ringed on our calendar and we are busy selling the expendable and keeping the sentimental. We are seasoned veterans at this sort of thing and it feels like we are on top of everything. There is no anxiety about leaving. On the contrary, I am excited: equally pleased to be leaving Sri Lanka and to be moving to the States. Every time we sell something, it feels that we are one step further along from shedding this life and preparing for the next. Our TV has gone, to be replaced with an old portable borrowed from a friend for the last month. Our bed has been sold, but the buyer let us keep it until we are ready to leave. Mary's moped has been sold and will be collected next week. The sofa, the computer, all our cushions, i-pod, vacuum cleaner: all sold. Sam has stoically been through all his toys and clothes and sorted out all the things that he wants to keep and all the things that are going to a local orphanage. I am very proud of him. Mary and I are taking the things to the orphanage next week.

As a final treat, we are going to Unawatuna for the last time at the end of the month. Unawatuna is our favourite place in Sri Lanka: a small and beautiful, classical bay of white sands and palm trees near Galle. It is a bit rustic, more of a back packer destination than a resort. There are no luxury hotels there, just guesthouses that sit on the edge of the beach. The rooms are basic, some have air conditioning, most have a ceiling fan, but the heat is always less intense here because of the lovely cooling wind that blows in from the Indian ocean. There are many lovely beaches in Sri Lanka, but at the vast majority of them the swell of the ocean is too dangerous for much of the year. Sri Lanka has a lot of ocean off the east and west coasts, but off the south coast there is no land until you get to Antarctica, more than an earth hemisphere away. Therefore, the waves that crash in all over the south coast tend to make bathing too dangerous. The exception seems to be at Unawatuna where the bay and coral reef act as a natural barrier and keep the more dangerous surf away.

We are staying at the Villa hotel, a strangely shaped narrow guesthouse with just three rooms piled on top of one another with balconies overlooking the ocean. The rooms are basic and small with an air conditioning unit, a small TV and a fridge, but the real reason you stay there is for the views over the beach and the ocean, less than thirty feet from the front of the guesthouse. Breakfast is served on small wooden tables in the sand in front of the guesthouse where waves occasionally roll in enough for the surf to gently reach your feet. And the price of this heavenly idyll is less than forty US dollars a night for all three of us — breakfast included. We have been to Unawatuna so many times that people recognize us and know us. The locals who run the Happy Banana, the Lucky Tuna, the Tartaruga Bar, or the Peacock all greet me with, 'Mr. Harry, you are back!', which says a lot about how much time I spend in their bars while we are down there.

Unawatuna has had its share of misfortune. It was badly affected in the 2004 Tsunami and all of the locals have harrowing tales of the day. In nearby Galle, thousands of people were killed. The owner of the Full Moon in Unawatuna tells a story of how he survived by clinging to the wooden door of his room as he was swept along for a mile inland by the huge tide. Everyone who survived has a similar tale, of how luck favoured them that day, how an innocent or frivolous decision kept them away from somewhere that was destroyed by the wave. Six years later there are still signs of the destruction that occurred that day: destroyed walls, or shells of homes are common and there are enormous graveyards all along the coast, some with elaborate gravestones, but many others with two pieces of wood roped together in simple cross. And these represent only the Christians that died that day. The vast majority of the South of Sri Lanka is of course Buddhist, and they chose cremation.

Thankfully, it seems the good times are returning to Unawatuna. We have noticed more and more tourists visiting over the last year. There were times in the middle of the conflict when we would have the entire beach to ourselves, save for a few others visiting from Colombo who we invariably knew. We could turn up at the beach and within five minutes Sam would have found someone from his school. But over the course of the last year, rooms have been increasingly difficult to book as more people visit. It is good for the economy, but we also feel that it is perhaps appropriate that we are leaving now, before all our wonderful memories of the beach become soured by the inevitable commercialization that will happen.

We have given up on the train these days and we usually take the road to Unawatuna. This involves getting on a minibus to Galle from Fort bus station. We get the air-conditioned minibus which means we have to pay more but it still works out at less than a six dollars for all three of us for what is a three-and-a-half hour ride. The air-conditioned minibuses tend to play loud Indian music from indeterminable Bollywood movies that everyone in the bus knows except for us and they hum and sing along in falsetto to the tune. The driver touts for business for the entire journey so that when he is not driving dangerously fast on the Galle road he is screeching to a halt to cram another paying customer on board. Whatever the legal maximum number of passengers is for one of these buses, we always greatly exceed it. Whenever the regular seats are full, 'extra' seats appear, to be opened up in the aisle, pulled out from the side of the regular seats. People cram themselves onto the front bench so tightly that the driver needs to squeeze his arse between his seat and the angle of the door. The exit area around the door is crammed with four or maybe five standing passengers and the gap of oil stained carpet that separates the front cabin from the seats in the rear provides room for five or six kids to sit unprotected and cross legged in front of the big windscreen. The aisle seats mean that once you are seated there is no way to reach the front of the bus once we are on the move unless you are prepared to climb over everyone's head. And if someone wants to get off before the scheduled stop in Galle, climb over everyone's head is exactly what you must do. They grab their bags, push on shoulders, climb over heads, stand on laps and clamber to the front as the driver continues to tear along the road. And no one ever complains. On one occasion, we were all heading south for the weekend at the beach when the bus backfired, the engine belched black smoke and the driver was forced to quickly pull over by the side of the road. He jumped out, took one look at the engine and told everyone to get off. He gave us back half of our money, for we had made it roughly half way there, and then walked off in the direction of Colombo. After a few confused glances around, the passengers shrugged and started trooping off in the opposite direction, towards Galle, until we could flag down enough minibuses to accommodate the thirty or so of us stranded on the roadside.

33

Gotabaya Rajapaksa, the President's brother, defence secretary and all round bad guy, threatened to have General Fonseca executed today. In an interview with the BBC no less.

General Fonseca has long maintained that Gotabaya Rajapaksa ordered army officers to shoot and kill surrendering Tamil Tigers at the end of the war. Fonseca has also claimed that there is an eyewitness to this, said to be a Sri Lankan journalist who is now in hiding overseas. Fonseca has already said that he would be prepared to testify before any independent investigation of alleged abuses during the Tamil war, promising that he 'will not hide anything'.

When this was put to Gotabaya by the BBC, he threatened to have the General executed for treason:

'He can't do that', he said. 'He was the commander. That's a treason. We will hang him if he do that. I'm telling you... How can he betray the country? He is a liar, liar, liar.'

Gotabaya then went on to rule out any possibility of an independent investigation of alleged war crimes in the final phase of the war, claiming that the Government had the ability to 'investigate all these things'. He insisted, in his peculiar high pitched effeminate voice, that no civilians were killed by the army at the end of the war, despite the UN and many international non-government organisations saying there were tens of thousands of civilian deaths.

For his part, Fonseca has maintained that he wants to expose war crimes and that he would be a traitor to his country only if he hushed it up. Without question, the Rajapaksa/Fonseca feud is set to continue. It would be interesting if that Sri Lankan journalist, the eye witness currently in hiding, came forward to corroborate Fonseca's claims. It would take a brave individual to do that though.

I wonder what the Tamils make of this unseemly argument? Since the end of the war, the new Tamil leadership has dropped the call for the independent state of Eelam and has asked instead for federalism and some measure of self-governance. They have stated that they aim to do this in a non-violent manner. If you consider that around the major Sri Lankan city of Jaffna the Tamils represent 95 per cent of the population and around Trincomalee they represent 70 per cent, the demand does not, to me, look to be asking for too much.

If there is not to be a repetition of the demand for their own state, and the inevitable conflict that will result, then surely the Government needs to properly address integration and introduce at least a degree of self-determination for the Tamil people. Yet the President has already ruled it out completely. Surely, a third party, independent and transparent enquiry into the alleged atrocities committed against innocent Tamil civilians at the end of the conflict would go a long way to fostering some much needed national reconciliation. Yet Gotabaya, perhaps for obvious reasons of self-preservation, will not entertain the idea.

There seems to me to be very little reaching out to the Tamil people. The State of Emergency has just been confirmed again, clearing the way for continued indiscriminate army checkpoints, while the Government maintains its irrational dual notion that it has on one hand defeated terrorism but on the other it is still at risk from 'Tamil organisations overseas' and 'traitors at home'. For good measure, the Victory Day parade that was washed out in the monsoon has been rearranged for next week and the President will undertake a special War heroes commemoration in the Parliament grounds. At the moment the Sri Lankan government is imposing a military style settlement on the Tamil people.

The President is currently in India on an official visit and Manmohan Singh, the Indian Prime Minister, is expected to raise the issue of self-determination for the Sri Lankan Tamils. He has to — the huge province of Tamil Nadu in Southern India shares the language, religion and culture of the Sri Lankan Tamils and there have been demonstrations there at the perceived injustices of the Singhalese. Yet, India is caught in a strategic quandary. It has a natural empathy for the Tamil people, but it is well aware that any criticism of Sri Lanka could accelerate Chinese/Sri Lankan cooperation, increasing China's already sizable interest in the Indian Ocean. The only losers as far as I can see are the Sri Lankan Tamils. If history is any sort of guide, then it will not be too long before a new radical Tamil leadership forms to counter this heavy handed approach. I think the conflict will renew unless Singhalese mindsets change.

34

Although the manic monsoon is over, we still get subjected to the occasional torrential downpour and I got caught in one this morning when I walked to the tuc-tuc drivers at the end of the street so that one of them could take me to the supermarket. The skies were black and the thunder was rumbling away, so it was obvious that the rains were coming, but it is only a two minute walk to the tuc-tucs and I thought I could make it. I was within twenty yards of the sole remaining tuc-tuc at the corner when the heavens opened with incredible force. The rain was bouncing back up of the ground it was falling so heavily.

I ran towards the tuc-tuc and as I got closer some old man in the back seat starting yelling at me to come and get shelter. I jumped in the back next to him and we both started yanking down the tarpaulin rain flaps that are standard on the side of every tuc-tuc. We pinned and zipped the flaps shut and then sat there in our tiny sheltered vehicle while the torrential rain battered the roof and quickly flooded the street.

'Do you know where the driver is?' I asked the old man.
'No sir'
This was not that unusual. The drivers were always wandering off when they had parked up on the corner and it was common

for people to sit in the back and have a rest on the seats if they were not being used. I assumed that this old man had just been walking down the street, got caught in the rain like me, and managed to jump in for shelter just before I got there.

We had a little chat about the football world cup that was about to start but I quickly realized that he was not a football fan when he told me he wanted Liverpool to win.

We sat for around ten minutes, mostly in silence, as the rain continued to pound hard. To break the silence the old man would occasionally say, quite unnecessarily: 'it is still raining, no?' and I would ask him again if he knew where the driver was, to which he continued to shake his head.

Ten minutes later and the driver had still not appeared, but as the rain was still falling hard, I assumed he was taking cover somewhere. I decided that I would run for home and come back later when the rain had stopped. I started to unzip the side of the tuc-tuc rain flap and turned to say goodbye to the old man, explaining that as there was no driver, so I was going home.

'Wait' he said. 'I am the driver!' and he jumped into the front seat started the tuc-tuc engine and drove off quickly down the flooded road with me in the back, wondering why had he not set off twenty minutes ago if he was the real driver.

'Is this your tuc-tuc?' I asked, "I have not seen you around here before'

'Yes sir, I am the driver, where do you want to go?' he said as he crashed through puddles and swerved around manhole covers spewing excess water. He leaned so far forward that his nose was resting against the windscreen because the rain was too great for the flimsy windscreen wiper to cope. I shrugged and asked him to head for the local supermarket.

As I walked inside a Sri Lankan women began insisting loudly that she be served at an empty till because there was a sign that said 'Next Customer Please', even though there were only two checkout girls and they were both working at the two other tills. The manager came out and explained that the sign was always there, it did not mean anything. 'But it says Next Customer Please' repeated the woman and she instructed her driver to unpack all her groceries at the empty till. The Manager was pleading with the woman to please join another queue but she was having none of it. She was still there, being ignored by all the staff and the Manager, when I left. Respect lady, but there is a time to admit defeat.

The strange tuc-tuc driver had thoughtfully parked next to a deep puddle so I was soaked through when I got back into the tuc-tuc. I asked him if he would call next at a beer shop which was a few hundred metres behind us on the same road, and he immediately U-turned headfirst into the oncoming traffic and drove the wrong way down the busy road in the pouring rain. He tutted at the other drivers as they beeped furiously at us and he looked disbelievingly at a bus driver who shouted insults at him as he passed. 'What is the problem?' he kept repeating to himself. 'What is the problem?'

When we got back to the street corner by my house the rain had abated slightly and one of the regular tuc-tuc drivers was waiting in a panic under an umbrella, looking frantically up and down the street. As soon as he saw us come round the corner he rushed out and flagged us down. I sat in the back as he had a long and heated conversation with my driver in Sinhala. I had no problem imagining what the topic of conversation was.

'Do you know this man?' asked the regular driver.

'No — but he told me he was the driver' I said.

'He is no bloody driver' he said, and I walked the rest of the way home, with the regular tuc-tuc driver kicking the fake driver repeatedly up the backside behind me.

35

The football world cup is up and running in South Africa, although sports fans in Sri Lanka are far more excited about the Asia Cup, a cricket tournament between Sri Lanka, India, Pakistan and Bangladesh, which starts today. This year Sri Lanka is hosting the tournament which has added to the excitement. I would normally go to some of the games, but none of them are being played in Colombo: they are all being played in Dambulla, in Central Province, over 100 miles and at least five hours away. The stadium they are playing in is brand new and the builders have boasted that it only took them 167 days to complete it. That is another reason not to go in my opinion. I have seen Sri Lankan building sites and I do not want to spend much time in a structure that has been rushed to completion.

I love football and cricket equally, and so for me, cricket has been one of the plusses of living in Sri Lanka. We have five cricket channels on the TV and I have watched touring teams from India, England and New Zealand. Last year, there was a test match between Sri Lanka and India at the P. Sara Stadium in Colombo, which is less than a mile from our house and where I used to use the swimming pool (it was where I had that run-in with the wanker who scolded me for not showering before I got in the water and then told me that I was only a guest in his country).

Hosting the test match was a coup for the cricket stadium as it was the first time in a number of years that it had been chosen to host an international match.

On the eve of the game I went up to the stadium to see how they were preparing and walked straight onto the pitch and over to the nets where the Indian team was practicing. Most of the time I find that Sri Lanka is a dysfunctional nightmare, but there are occasions when living here really does pay dividends. Not one person asked me for a pass or an ID, and here I was, standing right behind Sachin Tendulka, the best batsmen in the world, in the nets, watching him dispatch a succession of first rate Indian bowlers all round the training area. When Sachin had finished I walked back with him and the other cricketers to the main stand and then wandered unopposed into the press room and joined a throng of journalists standing around the Indian captain Anil Kumble as he conducted a pre-match press conference. When this was over, I turned back to the ground and watched the Sri Lankans go through their fielding and slip catching drills on the other side of the outfield before wandering right out into the middle of the pitch to watch the South African TV engineers fix the stump camera and watch the local groundsman finish off painting the match sponsors logo on the grass. Can you imagine trying to do all this at Lords or the Oval?

Another huge plus is that the matches only cost around 5 US dollars for the best seats in the ground so I go to most of the matches that are played here. The atmosphere inside the ground ranges from funereal to chaotic, depending on who is playing and what format the game is played in. For example, test matches are not popular. I went with Sam to see a test between Sri Lanka against Pakistan, also at the P. Sara stadium, and there must have been less than one thousand people watching. I am pretty certain we were the only white people in the ground.

We spent most of the time waving to ourselves on the jumbo screen because the TV camera man hovered around Sam and filmed him during all the over breaks. Mary told me later that she was having a management lunch in a restaurant in Colombo when she suddenly saw Sam and me pop up on the TV in the corner, grinning and waving a big Sri Lankan flag at the screen.

While Test matches are quiet and staid affairs, One Day Internationals are a different matter entirely. They are so manic that I would not take Sam to one for fear of losing him in the throng. I went to a One Day game between Sri Lanka and India at the biggest stadium in Colombo, the Premadasa stadium. The stadium is named after Ranasinghe Premadasa, an ex-Prime Minister and President of Sri Lanka and Old Man Premadasa has an interesting history. He was the first President that came from a modest background, which immediately alienated him from the Govigama caste families who had ruled the country since independence. In addition, he also faced the problem of thousands of Indian Army peace keepers in the north of the island who had been invited in by his predecessor, JR Jayawardene. This was in the late eighties and the Indians had been invited to keep the peace as an independent third party between the Tamil Tigers and the government forces, but soon it became apparent that the arrangement suited nobody. The Indians tried to isolate the Tamil Tigers by arming different Tamil groups and so the Tamils Tigers had engaged in a bloody war against the Indians. Yet because the Indian presence on the island was so unpopular across Sri Lanka as a whole, there were numerous reports that Premadasa had ordered a secret mission for the Sri Lankan government to arm the Tamil Tigers in their battle against the Indians. The Indians eventually left and the straight away normal hostilities resumed between the Tamil Tigers and the Sri Lankan government forces. Premadasa was killed a few years later by a Tamil Tiger suicide bomber at a May Day rally in 1993.

CULTURE SHOCK AND TIGER BOMBS

Officially the stadium named after him holds 35,000 but for the match I saw against India I would guess that at least 50,000 had made it inside. I had a ticket, but it remained unchecked inside my pocket as I joined the crush to get through the small, unmanned turnstiles. To my right, people climbed over fences and to my left others forced open a vehicle access gate and swarmed inside. I even saw one large man throw three or four small kids up and over the perimeter wall. They landed inside the stadium and then quickly ran off in different directions. Seat allocation had been totally abandoned. You simply found a free space and camped out there for the duration of the game. The aisles were blocked with people squatting on the stairs and others hung from the steel girders supporting the floodlights. There was music everywhere: hundreds of brass bands were dotted all over the stadium, separated by no more than twenty or thirty yards, so that a constant din of trumpets, horns and drums echoed around the stadium. Booze flowed all day, people danced and sang and waved their flags and every once and a while the unmistakable whiff of a spliff floated down from nearby. Every boundary was met with frenzied flag waving, horn blowing and cheering. Every Indian wicket was greeted with hysterical jubilation, dancing and singing. An army of hot dog and beer salesmen climbed between people and over seats to serve their refreshments and when things got desperate, because there was no way to leave your seat and find it again, people peed into empty coke bottles and beer cans and hurled them around the stands. It was chaotic and wonderful. I came home with a throbbing head from a combination of too much beer and outrageous exposure to brass bands, and smelly clothes from a day of sweating in a crowd that occasionally sprinkled me with piss.

On a final sporting note, I met an English bloke in a bar recently who was here doing some business in Sri Lanka but he told me that he intended to get back to the UK before the football world cup started. We had a bit of a chat about

England's chances, which we both agreed were typically slim. As he got up to leave, the English bloke said that his wife was heavily pregnant and if she dared to give birth during the world cup like she did during the last one four years earlier, then she could go to the hospital on her own because he had missed four live games.

I asked him what he had had last time, and straight as a die and deadly serious, he said, 'a tenner on Italy'.

36

The Victory Parade went ahead today but because of security concerns the area was sealed off and the general public was kept away. The army paraded up and down the street with their armoured vehicles and a wide variety of weapons all for the benefit of the President and his family. Everyone else had to watch it on television. I marked it as 'Victory to the Fascist Bastards Day' on our family calendar, but Mary changed it to 'Stay Away from the Galle Road Day'.

Rajapaksa spoke to the troops and he told them to ignore those who had accused them of human rights abuses. He made it sound like the Tamils should be grateful that the Sri Lankan army came marching to their rescue. According to the BBC, he said that the troops 'went into battle carrying a gun in one hand, the declaration of human rights the other, as well as taking food for the liberated people of the north and full of human kindness in their hearts'. By implication then, I guess Rajapaksa is claiming that the photographic and video evidence of the Sri Lankan army executing surrendering Tamil rebels and their indiscriminate bombing of civilians and hospitals was all done in the best interests of the Tamil people.

That being the case, you would think that the government would welcome the recently announced UN investigation into human rights abuses by both sides at the end of the war. However, the opposite is true. The Sri Lankans government is livid, claiming that they are planning their own investigation into the matter and they do not need any interference. They have declared that the UN commission members will be denied access to Sri Lanka: they will not be issued with visas. Russia and China were both quick to support the Sri Lankans, making their own separate announcements that any internal investigation should be carried out the Sri Lankans, and not the UN. It is increasingly clear who Sri Lanka's new friends are.

To complete the anti-West rhetoric, the European Union offered a compromise deal to the Sri Lankans whereby it would extend the period of its preferential trade benefit if Sri Lanka agreed in writing to meet a well defined number of human rights related actions. It seemed to me to be an ideal opportunity for both sides to save face and potentially save thousands of Sri Lankan jobs in the garment industry. However, the Sri Lankans have announced that they will not 'bow down' to the EU conditions, that the demands amount to interference in their country and they shall be placed 'in the dustbin'.

The President played to the crowd. He shrugged off the decision, saying that they do not need the concessions. He said, 'If the EU doesn't want to give it, let them keep it. I don't want it. We have gone and explained what we have done'.

According to the BBC, in 2008, Sri Lankan exports to the EU totaled 1.24 billion euros, virtually all of which was down to the textile industry. How can this be a good thing for Sri Lanka?

37

We are getting close to leaving and the great sale of our expendable goods is gathering pace. It is nice in some ways to see the items disappear because it is a visual reminder that we are getting close to leaving. In other ways however, it is a pain in the arse. Literally. Our sofa has gone and we have to use Aravinda and Amali's furniture, which, though attractive, is so hard and uncomfortable that it is generally more comfortable on the floor.

We spent all weekend sorting out what we wanted to sell or leave behind and what we wanted to have shipped, because the shipping agents were due to pack our things today at 9am. However, Mr AJ Creasy and his Associates called me at 9.30 to say that they could not make it today and that maybe they will make it on Wednesday. I told him that all of our stuff is in boxes in the front room waiting for him to pick it up. He actually laughed at me down the line, telling me he will see me sometime on Wednesday.

To add to the pre-departure stress levels, Amali the landlady has started being awkward about money. When we arrived, because we are foreigners, we needed to pay our rent a whole year in advance. I cannot believe that this is standard practice, as we needed to get a loan from Mary's employer just to cover the huge annual rent payment. Because we did not know our exact leaving date a year ago, we paid Amali rent until the end of July. Now that we have settled on a departure date, we asked Amali to refund us the overpayment, which is around 250 dollars, but she just said that she had counted on keeping that money and therefore she did not want to give it back. She agreed to give us our refundable deposit back but then gave us 500 dollars instead of the 620 we were due. She wants to keep the difference for any bills that arrive after we go. The amounts are relatively small, but the principle is all wrong as far as I am concerned. I appreciate Aravinda and Amali are paying their children through expensive overseas universities but I still think she is being unreasonable. I have been brooding about it all day and in a fit of pique I have decided to get my own back. Without telling Mary, I have paid exactly 120 dollars less than I should have done on my last electricity bill, which makes us even. And, to take care of some of that overpaid rent I am leaving the immersion heater on for hours to leave a nice big electricity bill surprise for her after we have gone.

38

AJ Creasy arrived today and finally packed our things. Everything we own is in 33 boxes in his warehouse at the Colombo port awaiting the long journey to Wisconsin. 33 boxes worth does not seem like a great deal for 45 years worth of accumulation.

In any case, the packing seemed to go okay, although old Creasy did not get off to a good start. He waltzed into my house without an apology for being two days late, sat down uninvited on my living room floor, opened his newspaper packet of curry and rice and began shoving fistfuls into his mouth with his fingers. He was none too careful about it either as I had to later hoover up little remnants of his splattered curry and rice from the floor. The five packers he brought with him did not do any work while the boss was eating and they all sat on the floor in the dining room next to AJ Creasy, chatting to each other and smiling at me.

I wanted to crack the whip and get them working, but I was under strict orders from Mary not to start a fight with the shipping agents. AJ Creasy and his gang of five are the people we have entrusted with all our worldly goods and effects and we would like to get them all at the other end in one piece if at all possible.

So, I talked with AJ Creasy and provided drinking water for him and his five workers before they eventually got down to some work.

It looked as though they actually did a decent job. Certainly they were better than the agents who unpacked us when we got here and dropped our TV in the street, sending the screen into a million different pieces in all directions. The noise drew the attention of all our neighbours who came out to meet us. An unusual way to announce your arrival in a new country, I thought. When AJ Creasy packed up and left, I heard on the radio that there had been a minor panic in the Pettah area of Colombo earlier today. There had been a loud explosion and inevitably people had worried that the Tamil Tiger bombers might be back. Although the Government is always quick to congratulate itself on defeating terrorism in Sri Lanka, it is equally quick to identify the continued danger to the country that exists within the Tamil diaspora overseas. For example, the Government recently claimed that 25 out of the 76 Tamil men who tried to enter Canada last year were actually LTTE cadres and, more worryingly, three LTTE men had been captured in India with large quantities of detonators and explosives, which they planned to smuggle into Sri Lanka. Therefore, the radio was quick to announce that the explosion in Pettah this morning was not down to renewed hostilities with the Tamil community, but instead, was due to someone throwing a hand grenade during a personal dispute. A personal dispute?! A hand grenade!? The radio news announced this quite matter-of-factly, as though this sort of thing is quite common. Nine people were hospitalized.

39

As planned, we had a last lovely break in Unawatuna. The minibus trip (which set off from Pettah, no sign of any hand grenades today) was cramped but mercifully uneventful, although there did seem to be more than a normal amount of severe breaking and swerving. Perhaps it was down to the obscured view that the driver had due to the little boy that was sitting on his lap for the entire four hour ride. Either that or it was from the excessive paraphernalia that littered his windscreen and the top of his dashboard.

Most minibus and tuc-tuc drivers in Sri Lanka like to decorate their dashboard to some extent, but this driver had added so many distracting trinkets to the front of his minibus that his view was reduced to a fraction of what it should be. His windscreen was framed by a thick green plastic vine with luminous pink and yellow flowers and interwoven with all manner of fake shrubbery and big sparkling lights. Large and bountiful plastic bunches of purple grapes hung from the ceiling and swung down in front of the window at eye level so the driver had to continually bat them aside to see the road ahead. Stickers of the Buddha, of Bollywood actresses and a smiling Rajapaksa further decorated the windscreen and somewhere amongst all this adornment was the cardboard bus sign that announced that this was the bus from Colombo to Galle. Statues of Buddha were positioned along the top of the dashboard, their heads popping up and forming a silhouette along the bottom of the windscreen, and a big Wesak lantern hung and swung with pride of place in the centre of the window.

In the end we did not stay at the Little Villa on account of there being no roof when we got there. I had called the place two days earlier to make sure that we still had our booking, having learnt from prior experience that a confirmed booking does not necessarily mean a room being kept for your arrival. The owner of the Little Villa had told me proudly that his word was good and that he would not give my room to anyone else. He did not mention that the roof of said room was no longer there. Incredibly, when we arrived he still checked us in, gave us a key and then showed us to our room. As soon as we walked in, Mary, Sam and I looked up at the gaping hole with the afternoon sun shining through. The owner though made straight for a new box refrigerator he had had installed and made a big issue of demonstrating how effectively the door opened and closed and telling us how it was the latest model from India. He finished with the refrigerator demonstration and was about to move on to the various wonders of the TV when he could avoid eye contact with us no longer and he was forced to look upwards and acknowledge the obvious.

Reluctantly he told us that a big storm had blown through Unawatuna a week previously and had removed the Little Villa roof. He said that he was so relieved that it was only the low season otherwise his guests would be disappointed. He noticed Mary and I exchange an exasperated look at this point so he added quickly that he might be able to arrange a little discount on the account of there being a small problem with the roof. Such was the lack of protection afforded by the Little Villa roof that we decided to walk up the beach and see if there was anything else available. Luckily there were lots of spare rooms, because as the manager of the Little Villa had said, thankfully it was only the low season.

We found a room at a place just along the beach called the Banana Garden. Our man there rented us a room fitted with an air conditioning unit and a fan, but then charged us an extra ten dollars a night for the use of the remote control for the air conditioner. It may have been off season but it was also the Possun Poya weekend and as the Banana Garden man said, 'that being so, everything is more expensive for that, sir'. We were so relieved to have found a room with a roof that we splashed out and took the a/c remote control too.

Poyas in Unawatuna are unusual. They are unusual everywhere I suppose, but in Unawatuna they are particularly unusual. Most of the time Unawatuna is a tranquil beach where it easy to relax and unwind. The beach has plenty of space, there are usually a few tourists and one or two locals selling hand made crafts. The cheap bars scattered along the beach cater to just a few customers and the atmosphere is chilled, there is no pretension to be a party destination. However, every Poya the Sri Lankan people of Unawatuna hit the beach, hit the bottle and go wild. The rest of the month, when alcohol was freely available, the locals were quite restrained. But on a Buddhist spiritual day, when alcohol was banned, it was time to head to the beach in large numbers and get completely leathered.

Possun Poya was no exception. By mid morning the sea was full of drunken Sri Lankan men in their see-through white Y-front underpants, splashing and singing, while others congregated on the beach and took swigs from bottles of arrack. The younger boys stood around in tight circles, clapping and singing songs in Sinhala that sounded as though they would not be out of place at an English football match. Other groups banged drums and played trumpets, practicing the tunes that are played at all the local cricket matches. Both the old and the young alike drank far too much and passed out in the sand. Some got caught in the surf and rolled out into the breakers, but there was always someone on hand to pull them out of the water by their hand or their leg. There were some women at the beach too, but they were seriously outnumbered by the men, and they all looked quite sober. When they went in the sea they did so fully clothed. Some of the younger men tried to entice the girls by removing their underpants in the waist high water and waving them over their heads whilst whistling and cheering. But the girls ignored them and kept to themselves in sober groups. It all made tremendously entertaining viewing. There must have been three or four hundred Sri Lankans boozing and singing on the beach.

We stayed on the beach watching from a safe distance until a very drunk brute of man started slugging wildly at anyone who came near him. He could barely stand but he still took out three or four with indiscriminate windmill punches. Eventually he was sedated by a clobber on the head with a wooden boat oar and then dragged along the beach by his legs amidst great shouting and cheering, (it was like they were celebrating the slaying of a big Medieval giant), before being pushed into the back of a tuc-tuc where the driver sped off quickly in case he woke up.

40

We are in our last week in Sri Lanka. After months of waiting and time dragging, everything now seems to be happening too quickly. We still need to find a home for our cat Poppy. Ideally we would like to leave her here so that she can come with the house so to speak. I am pretty sure we could play on Amali's Buddhist tendencies here. She thinks all living things have a soul, she is always feeding the stray animals in the street and she always takes in the wounded birds that the cats half maim. It is also one of reasons why we had such an ant problem, Amali did not want to kill them.

However, I would surely jeopardize Poppy's future if I carried out my plan to underpay the electricity bill and leaving the immersion heater on for too long. Is it really that important? I need to consider further because I think I have the moral high ground, and, if it really came down to it, I am pretty sure the cat could look after itself in the street. There is plenty to live on out there after all.

There is one more financial issue I need to take care of before we go. I need to get my money back from the Ceylon Bottled Water Company. These people have delivered large plastic bottles of drinking water to our home for the last three years and they owe me a tenner. Their service has been good, every Tuesday at 10am a van pulls up and four kids carry the big bottles slung over their shoulder to my kitchen where we keep the water dispenser. When we opened the account they charged me twenty dollars as a 'foreigner deposit'. Sri Lankans do not need to pay any kind of deposit! When I told them that the concept of a 'foreigner deposit' was an outrageous discrimination, they promised me that I could have my money back when I returned the empty bottles at the end of the contract. Well, that time has come and I want my cash back. After they deducted my outstanding bills, they calculated that I was owed just over 1000 Rupees, the equivalent of around 10 US dollars. There is a man who comes every month on a motorcycle who collects my payments, so I assumed that he would return my deposit. However, it transpires that this fellow is not allowed to give money to the customer, he can only take it. I will have to go in person to the downtown office for my cash back. I make this sound all straight forward, but this information took me the best part of a day to acquire as the receptionist kept putting me on hold and then transferring me to non-existent customer service people, or sometimes just hanging up on me.

At one point I made it through to someone who promised me delivery of a cheque through the post in a week.

'No' I said, 'I have closed my bank account and I am leaving the country for good in a week's time'

'Oh' came the reply. 'We are in a real quandary then'. Then there was a long silence and they hung up.

Someone else at the company said that I could have a cheque if I came for it on the 10th of July, (even though I had made it clear that my last day in the country was the 6th). Each time, rather than attempt to solve the problem, the person hung up. Customer service in the third world is one non-stop frustration. The third phase of culture shock! Eventually someone, (nobody would give me their name), said that if I came to the office then I could have cash - not a cheque - cash. But, I had to go down there in person. So later today, I am going for my cash. It is a principle thing now.

41

Ceylon Bottled Water Company are complete and utter bastards. I went down there for my deposit, and their 'head office' is not easy to find, tucked away in a side street off R. A de Mel Mawatha, on the sixth floor of a urine stinking office building with no elevator. Their receptionist, who I have to say was very friendly, in stark contrast to her telephone manner, asked me to take a seat and then seemed to forget about me for the next thirty minutes, despite us being the only two people in a closet sized reception room.

I am well accustomed to waiting around for things in Sri Lanka, it is what you have to do, but after half an hour I asked the receptionist what the hold up was. She said that she would check and disappeared behind a door. There was no sign of her for the next ten minutes so I opened the door and I saw her sitting on the edge of a table just inside, chatting to some of her colleagues. I coughed loudly to get her attention and I gave her a raised eye brow what-is-going-on look, but she simply shrugged and smiled and continued with her discussion with her friends.

I returned to my seat and waited another ten minutes or so until eventually a different young girl came out.

'Mr Harry?' she asked
'That's me'
'You are wanting your deposit back?'
'Yes please'
'It will be a little waiting time as the man who signs the cheques is in a meeting' she said.
'I don't want a cheque. I want cash. You know, I have been through this many times.'
'Ah, you want cash? Okay, please sit' she said and quickly disappeared behind the door.

I decided that from now on I would not sit down as maybe they thought that I was comfortable and quite happy to keep on waiting. The receptionist came back out to her desk and seemed quite perturbed that I did not want to sit down. Every few minutes she looked up from her desk and asked me if I wanted to sit down. Each time I shook my head and said I only wanted to get my money and go. A few minutes later she would ask me again to sit down and I would refuse. And so on, and so on.

Eventually a different woman again came out from behind the door.

'Mr Harry?'
'Yes'
'You can collect your cash next week' she said with beaming smile. 'I am the accountant and we will have it for your collection on the eleventh of July'
'Look' I said 'I have explained this a hundred times. I am leaving the country on the sixth of July. Tomorrow.'
'Oh, then I will issue a cheque, if you please sit, I can....'
'NO. I need cash. My bank account is closed'
'That is right' chirped in the receptionist. 'His bank account is no longer open and he cannot take a cheque'
'Thats right' I said, pointing at the receptionist. 'See, she knows! I need cash.'

The accountant looked disappointed. 'Mr Harry, I am afraid there is a problem. Only the manager can authorize a cash payment and he is in America until the tenth of July'.

'What about the guy in the meeting?' I asked. 'The one who can write a cheque?'

'But I thought you didn't want a cheque' said the accountant.

'Yes, your account is closed' said the receptionist.

'No, I don't want a cheque!' I said. 'But can the man in the meeting not authorize a cash payment for me? You said he could write a cheque. Can he not give me cash?'

'No that is not going to be possible sir' said the accountant. 'The man who can write the cheque is not authorized to give out cash. These functions are kept quite separate for good and proper accounting practices'

'Ok, can I speak to the manager'

'No sir, he is in America'

"Ok, the man in the meeting. What about him?'

'He is no longer here, Mr Harry. He has gone'.

'But I have been sitting here for the last hour' I said. 'No one has come out there except for you and one other lady who tried to give me a cheque'.

'Oh, well, we have a back exit. He must have taken that route sir.'

I looked at the receptionist, who quickly gazed at the floor, and then I looked at the accountant, and she gave me a shrug.

'I only want what is mine' I said quite disconsolately, and they both murmured that they were sorry.

The three of us stood in silence for a few moments. Me contemplating what to so next. I wanted some kind of justice.

'Right then' I said quite abruptly, 'I'll have this instead then' and I quickly swiped a stapler from the receptionist's desk.

'No, Mr. Harry, you can't be taking things like this' said the accountant.

'And this!' I said and picked up cardboard desktop calendar with a scenic picture of the tea country hills on the front.

'Mr. Harry, please put these things back' she said from behind me but I was already marching out the door, looking around furtively for something else to swipe.

Then I saw it. The item I would take to make us even. Gazing down from the wall and grinning like a Cheshire cat was a two foot square framed picture of the President.

The accountant followed my glance and shot me a stern warning look: 'No — Mr — Harry—' she said slowly. 'you cannot take the picture, you must not take the ....'

'And I am taking Rajapaksa too!' I shouted, and hooked the cheap frame off the wall, stuck it under my arm and barged out the main door.

42
6 July 2010

Nothing ever happened about my little melt down at the Ceylon Bottled Water Company. Although the driver who was waiting outside for me did look a little surprised at the sight of me jogging down the street towards him with a framed picture of the President under my arm. I told him that they gave it to me as a present.

Mary was quite surprised by my new acquisition too, asking me why I had bought it when I was clearly not a fan of Rajapaksa, and why I had picked out one that was clearly not new: the glass panel was scratched and the frame was dusty. I could see that she was not convinced by my tale that I thought it would be the perfect souvenir and I had got it from a little shop in Borella. Luckily, the Ceylon Bottled Water Company did not call me or the police, probably because the only man who could make the decision was still in America. Mary did not push it in the end, we had too much to accomplish on our last day and the picture fitted in the suitcase without too much trouble.

I felt a little childish about the whole swipe the President scene, so I promptly paid the electric company the full amount for their bill and turned off the immersion heater. With Karma-like coincidence, Amali called round shortly afterwards to say that she would look after the cat and that she would try to rent the place with Poppy included. Our last concern has been taken care of. We are now all set to leave.

I thought that I would spend part of my last day in a tuc-tuc doing one last tour of the city. The driver set off at great speed and drove down Horton Place, over Kynsey Road and down past the Coffee Bean, where I used to go purely for the air conditioning in the heat of pre-monsoon March and April. We swung right and passed Odel, the shop that the snobs of Colombo loved to hang out at and I hated, we circled Viharamahadevi Park, the place where the snoggers hung out, and then we drove past Beira Lake and the Trans Asia hotel, the scene of the great stand off between General Fonseca and the government forces after the election, and the hotel that shook when the Tamil Tiger plane crashed into the tax office next door. We passed the Galle Face hotel, the place to see before you die, and the army barracks, tanks, checkpoints and guns and then we sped along the Galle Road with the buses, up to Majestic City, the spectacularly misnamed shopping centre, often referred to as 'Rat City' by Sam because of the huge rats we often saw scurrying around the underground car park. We headed back for home along Bauddhaloka Mawatha, past the huge new Chinese embassy, and then alongside the cemetery and back to Borella. It was a nice trip, an overdue moment of taking in the city without having a destination, and a fine way to spend my last morning in Colombo.

When we passed the UN office in town we had to dodge some unruly looking crowds waving Sri Lanka flags being led by a man with a loud speaker. The leader of the mob turned out to be the Housing Minister, Wimal Weerawansa, a close friend of the President, and he was demonstrating against the UN decision to appoint an expert panel to look into the alleged war crimes committed at the end of the civil war.

Later that day the police moved in to break up the demonstration and there were some nasty clashes as the police tried to escort UN staff in and out of the building. At that point Weerawansa called the President's brother, Gotabaya, and put him on his speaker phone where he ordered the police to step aside and allow the protesters to continue. Not surprisingly, the UN were extremely pissed off. The secretary-general closed the office and recalled his envoy to Sri Lanka, labelling as 'unacceptable' the manner in which the Sri Lankan authorities had failed to prevent the disruption of the work of the UN personnel in the country and had stood by and allowed the protests and demonstrations outside the UN office.

As if this was not dramatic enough, Weerawansa announced that he would immediately commence a hunger strike in protest at the UN investigation.

'I am starting a fast till death' he said, lying on a mattress outside the main gate of the UN office. 'Only when the accusations of war crimes are withdrawn and the panel abolished, will I stop this'.

The BBC reported that there was a photograph of UN Secretary-General Ban Ki-moon pinned to a tree nearby with insulting captions stuck on it and that nearby there were pictures of the three senior UN officials who will serve on the advisory panel labelled 'the three idiots'. By the end of the day the crowd set light to an effigy of the UN secretary general, Ban Ki-moon. It was all completely bananas, and somehow it seemed like a fitting episode to cap our final day in Sri Lanka.

With Mary and Sam having their last days at work and at school respectively, and having farewells with their friends and colleagues, after my tour of the city I thought I would wander along to say bye to my acquaintances from the last three years. The tuc-tuc drivers at the end of the street all shook my hand and wished me good luck in America. The drunk on the wall in the cricket shirt shouted 'Bye Bye, my Darling!' and waved his bottle of kassippu, to sniggers all round. Even the toad man got up off his stool and waddled over to say good bye. I think it was the first time I have seen him on his feet in three years.

When I left the house and began my walk to collect Sam from school that afternoon, word had obviously got round that we were going, presumably from the tuc-tuc drivers, because Mr. Green Peas shook my hand profusely and said that he would miss me, which seemed to be overdoing it a little, but he looked like he too had made an early start on the moonshine. I bumped into Semen, (named after the great Arsenal goalkeeper, and not jizz), still decked out in a full Arsenal football strip and football boots, and he said that he had heard we were going and he wanted to say goodbye. Even the monk from the temple at the end of the road acknowledged me without an evil stare for once. He nodded his head, raised his hand slowly to indicate that we should stop, and then asked me to pass on his farewell and best wishes to my 'good lady wife'.

Returning through the golf course on the way home from the school, we bumped into 'I'll get it' and we had one last reminisce with him about the cobra. Then he told me about the latest animal in his care, a purple heron, which he said he had started to care for after the accident. Curiosity got the better of me and I asked him what accident he was talking about. As quick as a flash, like a magician unveiling his assistant from underneath a cloak, 'I'll get it' whipped away a jute sack at his feet to reveal a huge purple heron lying motionless on its side. It was quite still, but obviously alive, as I could see one of it's eyes blinking nervously. It was at least three feet long with a beak like carving knife. Sam and I stepped back out of range.

'What's wrong with it?' I asked, slightly alarmed.

'This is a purple heron, sir'

'Yes, it's, erm, big, isn't it? Why is it lying still on it's side like that?' I asked.

'That is on account of the accident, sir' and he pointed to the heron's reed-like legs.

The bird had lost one of its thin legs, from just below the knee joint. It was a one and a half legged purple heron.

'This one was hit by a golf ball, sir. The tee shot went low and blasted away one of the legs. It popped and snapped, sir' and 'I'll get it' made some convincing heron leg snapping noises as he mimed the whole story, from golf swing to leg snap. The heron watched all this through his one big beady eye whilst lying still on the ground. The poor thing looked terrified.

'So, what are you going to do with it?' I asked.

'I have called for one of the caddy boys', he said . 'He knows all about these birds'.

(What, the caddy knows all about one legged purple herons? In any case, don't these birds spend all of their time wading around in the water looking for food?)

'But it can't walk anymore, can it? I mean, it's leg has snapped off' I said. 'What can the caddy boy do?'

'Ah but we have the other part of the leg here sir,' and 'I'll get it' rummaged around in the undergrowth next to the bird and produced the lower end of the poor birds's leg. It had been a clean snap. The bottom half of the leg was like a long reed, with a dangly webbed foot on the end. 'I'll get it' starting waving it around in front of us like Harry Potter trying out a new spell.

'If we cannot be sticking on this leg for him, the bird still has these' 'I'll get it' said as he bent down, rolled the poor bird onto its back and extended both of the heron's enormous wings. The bird lay there motionless, eyes bulging, as 'I'll get it' made big flapping motions with the wings. 'He is a bird. He has wings. No need for a leg!'

We did not want to hang around and watch the two of them try to stick a leg back on the heron so I wished 'I'll get it' the best of luck and shook his hand goodbye.

I have certainly had enough of the heat, humidity and frustrations of life in Sri Lanka, but I know that I am going to miss the various unexpected dramas that life can produce in this part of the world. Just when you think that you have seen it all, along comes a Government Housing Minister to embark on a hunger strike on a mattress outside the UN office and a hobbled purple heron with half a leg shot off by a golf ball. If I could have focused more on the fun and unpredictable things of living in Sri Lanka then I would have had more chance of accepting things for how they are and being fulfilled about living here. The mythical phase four of culture shock! But I cannot. There are too many irritations for me to get worked up about. The Ceylon Bottled Water Company, the shitty Post Office, the hopeless Police, the totalitarian President, the overzealous Army, the elitist society, the dangerous driving, the horrible hot and humid weather, the religious and cultural bigotry, and so on. I am stuck in phase three of culture shock and I know it. It is time to go somewhere where I have a chance of living a life without a constant barrage of drama and angst. Dare I say it, somewhere normal.

43
Madison, Wisconsin, United States, September 2010

Our new home is a rented apartment in a very cool American college town, Madison, the state capital of Wisconsin. Our personal effects arrived unscathed, thanks AJ Creasy, all is forgiven. Mary has found some work teaching, not enough to cover all our bills, but enough to cover our rent and groceries. It is a start, and as soon as I get permission, I am going to work too. It should all work out. Sam is thriving in the local elementary school and is now coming to grips with unfamiliar sports like baseball and American football. I have applied for my Green Card with the Department of Homeland Security, an organisation that sounds faintly sinister and who immediately finger printed me on my arrival in the country, but to date have not asked for any police certificates of good conduct, so all is well. Even Amali has been in contact to say that Poppy appears to be totally indifferent about us leaving Sri Lanka, as long as she gets her bowl of food each morning and night. Which is how it should be.

It feels good to be away from the chaos and turmoil of Sri Lanka but I am still drawn towards the South East Asia news section of the BBC website each day to follow events there.

I see that old Wimal Weerawansa did not last long with his hunger strike. He ended it after just three days. First he was visited on his mattress by Gotabaya and then by the President himself, who took a glass of water, pressed it to Weerawansa's lips and made him take a sip. Within minutes, Weerawansa had been rolled onto a stretcher and taken away in an ambulance while his supporters chanted his name and announced a whole raft of new religious ceremonies in order to bless him.

General Fonseca's woes continue to mount. The military court found him guilty on the charges of engaging in politics while on active service and of corruption involving arms deals. He was stripped of his rank, medals and parliamentary seat and sentenced to 30 months imprisonment with hard labour. On top of this, the government has charged him in the civilian court with an extra 21 charges of corruption and an additional charge of recruiting army deserters to help him in his failed presidential election campaign which could lead to an extra 20 years in jail. He still has to face the further charge of inciting unrest by accusing Gotabaya of war crimes. Even Fonseca's son-in-law is in trouble now. The government has charged him with other corruption charges, although he has wisely gone into hiding and is now on the run.

The harassment of journalists in the country continues. In August, twelve masked men, most of them armed, stormed Siyatha, a TV and Radio station in Colombo. They threw petrol-bombs and destroyed much of the broadcasting equipment, forcing staff to kneel at gunpoint and assaulting two of them. The station owner left the country some months ago after it emerged that he had supported General Fonseca during the presidential elections. The government had previously stopped Siyatha from covering official events and withdrew all advertising in its newspaper.

Rajapaksa's grip on the country is getting increasingly tighter. First, the cabinet backed a proposal to change the country's constitution to allow the President to run for a third term, removing the current limit of two terms. Then, shortly afterwards, the President introduced further constitutional amendments that allowed him to seek an unlimited number of terms, as well as other measures that would greatly increase his powers, such as letting him appoint all the top judges and commissioners for elections, and human rights and other affairs, unchecked by any legal veto.

With Rajapaksa's clear majority in the parliament, the new amendments were expected to be voted into law with ease. The Supreme Court have already cleared the draft bill and opposition MPs have claimed that bribes and threats were used to secure the votes and they have complained that the country is on the verge of a dictatorship. Rajapaksa's megalomaniacal mission has meant that there has been no national reconciliation that the country so desperately needs. It looks to me as though renewed conflict is more likely that sustained peace.

The framed portrait of Rajapaksa, the one I stole from the Ceylon Bottled Water Company, hangs on my wall in Madison. Mary would like me to take it down, and I will eventually, but at the moment it helps to remind me of what we have left behind, the chaos of Colombo. In Madison, it is a very pleasant 70 degrees and the leaves are turning orange and yellow. If I look out of the window here I can see trees sway gently in the cool autumn sunshine and kids playing in the street. One look up at Rajapaksa and I am reminded of the kid in Colombo punching his goat repeatedly on the side of the head and shoving him in a sack, or the torrential downpours and constant humidity and heat. Looking at Rajapaksa helps me to appreciate what we have here: an uninterrupted power supply; fast and reliable internet; a car and drivers that obey traffic rules; parks to play football in; supermarkets with plenty of goods, with aisles big wide enough for two trolleys to pass; orderly queuing with no cutting in; great customer service; salespeople who turn up when they promise to and no military road blocks. These are things I value, and I missed.

Everything is new and exciting and I am happy. This must be phase one of culture shock. But there is a difference. This time the country has a comfortable and familiar feel already and Madison feels like a place where we can settle down permanently. We have made new friends, (phase two of culture shock), and none of them hate Madison or want to book holidays out of the United States at the first opportunity. In fact, they all seem very happy here too. This is something new for us. For the first time in twenty years I think I am ready to call somewhere home and mean it.

Would you like to see your manuscript become a book?

If you are interested in becoming a PublishAmerica author, please submit your manuscript for possible publication to us at:

acquisitions@publishamerica.com

You may also mail in your manuscript to:

**PublishAmerica
PO Box 151
Frederick, MD 21705**

www.publishamerica.com

CPSIA information can be obtained at www.ICGtesting.com
Printed in the USA
LVOW06s0821051013

355509LV00002B/97/P

9 781456 060718